RECONNECTING

Super
HUSBAND

& *Wonder*
# WIFE

RECONNECTING

Super
HUSBAND
& *Wonder* WIFE

Kenn Kington

COPYRIGHTS

ACKNOWLEDGEMENTS

This project would not exists without God's gracious, patient hand guiding a clueless, hopeless guy into the reality of God's most wonderful truth. Thanks to God first and foremost for His individual, intimate, intricate grace and wisdom. This work would also not exist had God not brought the most wonderful wife in the world into my life. Heather is such a champion for living the truth. We worked through this material together when we met, during the dating stages and have been ever since. She is also an honest and gracious editor. Most of all, her input, encouragement and support helped make an overwhelming task a reality. Heather thanks for being my best friend and a beautiful example of what a wonder woman should look like.

A very special thanks is also in order for my project editor Theresa Druckenmiller. Her endless patience and gifted eye made this work so much better than I had even hoped. Her calm acceptance and focus of my many faults and tangents consistently kept this on course. She is a pleasure and joy to work with.

A special thanks to Shawn Schantz is also in order. His creative edit brought so much to the quality of the work you now hold. It was a pain-staking task to translate my talks into written form. Shawn made this process make sense. His talent as a writer is so impressive and refined. I am honored that he would take the time to invest that talent in this project.

Thanks also to the many friends who have given honest input, offered countless prayers, and encouragment. I can honestly say super men and wonder women surround me.

PREFACE

I am so impressed you took the time to read this section. To be completely honest, you have just clued into the most important aspect of this book—without having to wait until the end to figure it out! There is one element that is an absolute necessity for this philosophy to work in your marriage. I am going to spill the beans right here in the often skipped section called the preface. This secret element is simple, yet complex, and is discovered by understanding the class of reading this book is.

This book is NOT to be read and pondered. If intellectual and theological stimulation is your goal, pick up a copy of Plato and look for the hidden meanings. This book is written for one reason...finding the truths that make marriage workable and fulfilling.

The effectiveness of this book is based on one simple premise. YOU have to apply the truth. I wish it was as easy as thinking the right thoughts, talking to the right people, or agreeing with the right truth. It is not. The only way these principles will work is if you actively, passionately, purposefully, consistently (and any other "ly" ending words you can think of) Do It!!!

A note of encouragement. Rest assured that you will fall short, and it will not come to you naturally. (Wow, thanks for the boost of confidence?!). This quest is not for the passive or faint-hearted. This book is for people who desire real answers and solutions that work. The material covered is not a theologically profound work. It is a first hand encounter this writer had with God directing him (me) from a state of "cluelessness" to being happily married in a wonderful, growing relationship.

The magic is not found in the guidance of the words in this book, or in the examples of trials, shortfalls, and successes, yet hopefully they will be encouraging and helpful. The magic is in the encounter you will have with the living, loving God of all if you choose to learn and live these (His) truths. It will be a fun journey, and I look forward to hearing how God works in your life.

Here we go...

TABLE OF CONTENTS

Introduction 1

Section 1- Reconnecting Our Approaches 4

Chapter 1: Microwavable Minute Rice 8
Complete Commitment

Chapter 2: Sharing Tongues 14
Getting Real

Chapter 3: I Just Wanted to Be With You 22
Giving Unconditionally

Chapter 4: Big Macs and Vitamins 28
Fundamental vs. Supplemental Intimacy Needs

Section 2- Reconnecting Our Attitudes 38

Chapter 5: Lasting Love Absolutely Guaranteed 40
Secrets of Love: Expect Nothing and Appreciate Everything

Chapter 6: Road Map to Love 54
Defining and Becoming the Character of Love

Chapter 7: Where Am I? 60
Exact Directions to Complete Love

Section 3-Reconnecting Our Actions 66

Chapter 8: Becoming a Great Lover 68
Equations to Becoming a Great Lover

Chapter 9: Completely Trusting 76
Pursuit Principles

Chapter 10: How About Those Fries? 84
Personal Evaluation and Practical Application

INTRODUCTION

*O*nce I drove 23 hours just to spend an hour with my girlfriend. Yes, it was worth every ounce of the effort. Yes, we did eventually get married. I also remember winters' night few short years later in our first home. My bride of a few years asked me while I was walking into our bedroom if I would get her a blanket. I distinctly remember thinking but wisely not saying, "Are your legs broken?" Why couldn't she get it herself? Wow, how times change. This is the same woman. Over a few years I can honestly say I love her more today than the day I made the twenty-three hour journey. What changed?

Most every couple I have contact with can express a similar story or at least a similar feeling from time to time. The problem is when those feelings and thought become too frequent or worse, become the norm. It may be expressed in a multitude of ways. "I wish we were more like when we first got married." "You just don't appreciate all I do for this family." Sometimes even worse. It may be a feeling that never gets expressed due to the repetition. What good would it do? Too often we resolve ourselves to just endure the process and live for those moments that are good.

Those times of bliss can be more frequent and the possibility even the norm. It is not brain surgery. We had it all figured out when we first got married. We will just always be on a honeymoon because we are in LOVE. Why did that change? What happened? We are both still on the line it is just that one or both of us has a bad connection.

If you have ever experienced the frustration of trying to talk to someone on a mobile phone you know what I mean. Everything is fine and then the wonders of modern technology take over. "Can you hear me?" "Are you there?" "I can hear you." "There you are... No, I lost you." "If you can hear me call me back when you get a better signal." The worst though is talking for several minutes; the other party has long since lost the signal. When I pause for a response I realize I have been talking to NOBODY! I know several places on my commute home where I just forewarn the person, "I am about to lose you. I will call right back." When I know where the dead spots are it is much less frustrating.

This book is about finding those dead spots in a marriage and getting reconnected. Where has our attitude lost the signal without our realizing it? What have we done differently that causes our approach to lose it's strength. It seems so often I am putting in more effort and getting less connection with my spouse. Why? What actions am I taking to make our connection as strong as possible?

The answers will only come from you. It is my hope that the timeless truths shared from my experience and the questions at the end of each chapter will help you in the process.

SECTION ONE

RECONNECTING OUR
Approaches

I love chocolate-chip cookie dough ice cream. I love my wife. I love hitting a good drive on a par five. I love my four and a half pound Yorky named Polo. I love large ground beef pizzas. I love my mom and dad. What exactly is love? There are certainly different types, but what about the love deep inside I really desire? So often we say we want to recapture love, but to where did it escape? We invest great amounts of time, money, and energy seeking love. We risk hurt and embarrassment trying to grasp love. Yet, if we are honest, love felt differently while dating. Some ways better, some worse, but certainly different.

If we are going to experience lasting and genuine love, we must first learn, then embrace a biblically-based definition of love.

Before we dive right into the definition derived from months of study and application, let's work together for a moment and set our minds in that direction. This may be the only book you ever read where the first part is only two pages long, and **you** actually write this part. Rest easy that I will write the rest, but here is your opportunity and assignment. Define love. In your own words, what are the qualities that define love?

Love is:

What are some of the influences on your definition of love?

How is it different than when you were dating your spouse?

Now write how you think God would define love.

Are there any basic truths or biblical references you can note to support how you think God would define love? (List them here)

(STOP! Do not go on until you have written your part of this chapter.)

Now you can relax and enjoy the rest of the book.

Was it easy coming up with a definition of love? Does your definition and God's sound alike? If this exercise is not easy for you, take heart. Most people have a hard time putting into words what love actually is. How can we find lasting love when we are not really sure what it is? This is the starting point God brought me to after becoming open and honest with Him about my desire to learn and change.

The next few chapters will give the definition He laid upon my heart through numerous verses over several months. Your definition may have some of the same elements. Yours may have more to it or less, but the foundation must be there for us to experience the true definition of Love. What is LOVE? Love is...

CHAPTER ONE

Microwavable Minute Rice

Complete Commitment

*T*here it was, Kroger grocery store, aisle nine, top shelf. I wasn't looking for it, but it caught my eye for some reason. It was the perfect example of our society: <u>Microwavable Minute Rice</u>. Why did it catch my eye? It's just ironic that Minute Rice is no longer quick enough. Sixty seconds is now just too long to wait. We now need Microwavable Minute Rice!

Our society is an instant gratification society, an "I want what I want, when I want it, and how I want it" society. One of the main problems with most relationships today is that they don't meet this demand of instant perfection and are too often brushed aside. The large and growing majority of people today consciously live by this creed. The danger lies in the expectation of perfection without knowledge of how to truly love and care for our spouse. Possibly the most important element of Love is commitment, the opposite of this trend.

I often thought I wanted romance or the rush of feelings to be the center of a marriage, but I quickly found that those subjective aspects make a poor, shallow, and weak foundation. Many marriages have become boring or predicatable due to a foundation built on feelings. We must start with commitment, build on commitment, and constantly revisit commitment if there is to be any long term success in a relationship. Scott Peck's book, <u>*A Road Less Traveled,*</u> puts it beautifully. He shares the concept that the end of romantic love is not the end of love at all; rather it is the beginning of genuine love. Where feelings fade, commitment continues.[1]

We have too often tied the emotions involved with our natural hormonal reaction to the idea of love! The truth is that real love is defined quite differently. We will begin to discover love really is based on a conscious decision of the will rather than a fleeting feeling that may not decide to show up or stick around. The great part is when we do find that special someone who makes our heart flutter, and we make his or hers pound, and we agree to commit to each other. Please do not stop with the idea that love is only a commitment. Love is first a commitment.

I discovered what this commitment was all about one night around 2:30AM. Graham was about 19 months old and screaming in terror. As I entered his room the smell hit me before my eyes could focus on him sitting in his crib having just vomited everywhere. If you were to ask me my most LOVING memory of Graham's childhood I would NOT recount this instance. (It gets worse). The uncertainty in his eyes was so pitiful. He had never thrown-up and he was scared. When babies are scared they want to be held. Not after they are cleaned up. He wants to be held immediately. My heart led me through the process of cleaning him up and changing his sheets. After changing him and myself I thought I would put him back down and return to my own slumber. He would have nothing to do with that idea. In between sobs he would say, "Hold me!" This was not an option mind you it was an emphatic demand. I arranged the pillows on the guest bed and laid down with Graham on my chest. I wish it ended there and the precious memory would cease. He woke suddenly about an hour later; looked me in the eye and...another clean up was necessary. This happened about 5 time total during the next 4 hours. I finally figured out an escape plan from the path of future projectiles would be wise. After the second sickfest I had a system and had learned to minimize the cleanup. This is very gross! It is also the perfect example of the first component of love. I do not share this encounter with the romance and warmth we normally associate with love, but isn't it what love is? Real love. It doesn't sound good, or feel good, or smell good, yet we meet the needs of someone dear to us. Where the feelings stop real love starts. Where the feelings stop commitment reveals itself.

A biblical example is found in Luke 22:42. Jesus is in the garden praying the night before He was to be crucified. The only man to ever have perfect love expresses the entire concept of love being first and foremost a commitment. He asked the Father, "If you are willing, take this cup from me." With anguish that caused him to sweat blood, he begged this would not have to take place. Separation from the Father did not feel good or sound good, and it would be more painful than anything we will ever know. Yet, Jesus' commitment was so vivid when He proclaimed to the Father, "not my will, but yours be done."

This passage illustrated to me clearly that love is a commitment, not a feeling. When feelings are the foundation for love it will be shallow, short-lived, and increasingly frustrating. When Commitment is the foundation it provides an environment for feelings to go deeper, last longer and grow stronger with time. But, we can't stop with commitment alone. It is the foundation and is vital, but is not the only element. Truth be known, at times we are all difficult to live with.

When we do find ourselves in a relationship, there will certainly be times that we'll think we are with the most difficult person on the earth; sometimes they may feel the same. That is why commitment is imperative in every phase. Commitment is the key element no matter what stage you are in.

Our search for improving our marriages starts with defining love. We then have to sincerly ask do we really want to experience deep, lasting, growing love. Our response, "Of course we do!"

What we must realize is that this question cannot be answered with what we say, think, agreed with, argue, feel or aspire to do. The answer became clear and simple in the form of a straight-forward simple questions. "Am I committed to passionately pursuing what love really is? Will I focus my life on becoming what I find? Will I embody the qualities that are synonymous with God's definition of love?"

Reality is that what I study, ponder, articulate, discover, and even agree with mean next to nothing. The question you and I must answer if we are to find lasting love is, "Are we willing to commit to finding out the truth and diligently apply it in our lives?" So many people I meet take the absentee approach to the problem. They rationalize their strengths and ignore personal faults. It would be like complaining about the current politicians, but never exercising the right to vote. Multiply that and personalize it.

Countless people try to rationalize areas in their lives that are good and expect their marriages to benefit. I am personally guilty of this. I look to all my male friends and get overwhelming sympathy and support. They confirm, "You work hard, give of yourself. You are a great guy!" It gets worse in many cases when we try to overspiritualize. I tally all the votes in my one sided election and I win every time. The problem is I then go home and have to face the reality of my wife's one-sided election which she won by a landslide. Real progress will only be made when I come to realize the solution to the problem starts with "ME" not my spouse. I must commit myself to allowing God to work on me.

No aspect of our personal relationship with God is dependent on someone else to correct. The journey to being in a loving relationship starts in our own hearts regardless of our current situation. Are you ready to start the journey? If so, take a look at how God defines love. Read the following passages and consider these truths carefully.

1. Character of Love Philippians 4:8
2. Process of Love II Peter 1:5-7
3. Definition of Love I Corinthians 13:4-7

Now ask the question, "What qualities do I need to work on?" You may want to pray and ask God to show you where to start. When I asked, God simply said, "Pick one. You need work in all of them." He was right, and I still do.

Commitment is vital. We must be individually committed to putting what God says about love into action. What areas of life are we committed to? The second element of love answers that question and lies just ahead.

[1] Peck, Scott. <u>A Road Less Traveled</u>
(New York, New York. Touchstone, 1980,1998)

RECONNECTING

Discussion / Action
(approximate time 10 - 15 minutes)

1. Name 10 ways our society fosters immediate gratification (ex. microwave food).
2. Read Philippians 4:8-9.
3. How long does it take to develop and perfect these qualities?
4. Which quality mentioned in these verses do you feel is the biggest challenge for you personally?
5. Which of the qualities mentioned in these verses do you think your spouse best exemplifies?
6. Read I Corinthians 13:4-7 and answer questions 3, 4, & 5 again.
7. Pray for each other and thank God for the example your spouse provides. Pray for God to help you in your weak areas.

CHAPTER TWO

Sharing Tongues

Getting Real

I'm sure some readers have turned right to this chapter before reading anything else because of the catchy title. Some may think, "This is the part about relationships I really want to know about!" In an odd sort of way this could very well be the most important part of the Love definition. Allow me to briefly explain before we go straight to sharing tongues.

In Matthew 22:37,39, Jesus is asked to name the greatest commandment. He states clearly and concisely, "Love the Lord your God with all your heart, and with all your soul, and with all your mind." Jesus adds, "Love your neighbor as yourself." This condensed version of the entire Bible is a wonderful outline for the second element of our Love definition. It also answers the questions, "Where and how do I make a complete commitment to His truth in our relationship with Him and with others?" You may feel that it sounds much too simple. Not really!

People have become so overcome with their religion that they don't even know what they are saying and doing. To love God with all your heart, soul, and strength is not a religious agreement to attend Sunday school more often, sing in the choir, or tithe more faithfully. Those are certainly great disciplines, but loving is simply getting real, or being genuine and honest, with God on a very personal level.

One church in Florida has obviously missed this concept of being real as have many of us. I noticed this as I was on tour in the Sunshine State and driving with some friends to dinner. The radio played a well-meaning commercial from a local church proclaiming their benefits. They actually said, "Come to our church. We believe in sharing tongues!" Now I don't know about your worship preference, but when I go to church I don't care to share my tongue with anyone.

I had this bizarre picture in my mind of an usher at the door, handing out bulletins and greeting people with a holy kiss that was much more than scripture intended. They should have advertised on their marquee, "Please brush and floss before all services." To love God with all our heart is not to see how pious we can appear or how religious we can sound. Until we experience a relationship with God, we will not be ready to fully enjoy any other relationship.

God longs for us to get real with Him because of how special we are to him. Two of my favorite verses in all of the Bible are found in Psalms 139. Before we look at the verses, use your imagination for a minute. Picture yourself relaxing at the beach on a hot summer day. There is a gentle breeze coming off the water. The waves are crashing in the distance and you just sat down on your towel to dry off from a swim. Now take up a handful of sand. How many grains can you hold in your hand? Now look as far as you can up and down the beach. How many grains of sand can you see on the entire beach? Close your eyes and picture it. Millions... billions... trillions?

Yet in Ps. 139:17-18, David is getting real with God with all his heart and writes, "How precious to me are your thoughts, Oh God! How vast is the sum of them! Were I to count them, they would outnumber the grains of sand." Jeremiah 29:11-12, says, "I know the plans I have for you, declares the Lord, plans to prosper you and not to harm you, plans to give you hope and a future. Then you will call upon me and come and pray to me, and I will listen to you." If there is one thing we must grasp, it is God's overwhelming desire to provide our every need with His resources.

In addition to knowing a real God who cared enough to listen to my needs, my personal relationships needed a major dose of hopefulness for the future. It wasn't until I began to live like this was true that my relationship began to improve. We must get personal with God! We are admonished in I Peter 5:7 to cast all our anxieties upon Him because He cares for us. God and God alone can meet our needs, ease our fears, and fully understand our concerns.

It is time we fall hopelessly at His feet giving Him control of our lives, specifically our relationships, and put our hope and trust in Him. If you have never taken the time to pour out your heart to God, do it now. Become honest with Him. I had to get rid of a religious facade and tell God I was hurt, disappointed, and lonely. I also had to ask why it appeared He wasn't doing anything to help. That effort toward honesty opened the flood gates of insight. If we are to move forward, we must first come with a genuine heart to the Lord.

New Christians are probably best at getting real. They haven't had time to learn how to fake it. My favorite prayer of all time is from a few years back. It was straightforward and simple. I was traveling with a church on a ski retreat, driving in vans for six hours. Tired and starving upon arrival, we entered the only place in town still open – pizza!! (my favorite food on the planet). The wait staff began putting the modern day manna on the tables, and one of the starved students asked who would say the blessing. Finally, Mike, a new believer, spoke up and said, "I'll do it."

After a brief pause for the taking off of hats and grabbing of hands, it happened. From the bottom of his heart Mike prayed, "God we love pizza. Thanks!" That was it! I wish we could have seen our Heavenly Father physically. I am certain He was standing right there going, "Cool! I know you do!! Eat it!"

A pastor friend up north recounted a similar situation one night in his church. A recent convert was sitting on the front pew during the service. Very excited about his new freedom and filled with joy, he was a sight to see. The church did not know what was about to happen. The final prayer was spoken and the pastor in traditional form prompted the congregation with, "And all God's people said..." But before anyone could grunt the usual response, "Amen," this excited new brother yelled, "ALL RIGHT!" Three deacons fainted. This pastor shared with me that since then they close every Sunday evening service with the proclamation, "And all God's people said, ALL RIGHT!"

Jesus said, "Let the little ones come to me. Do not hinder them. The kingdom of God belongs to such as these."[1] We will not experience true love until we have come to be transparent and completely real before the all knowing, completely loving God. You never have to wonder what children are thinking or feeling. They wear it on their sleeves. God is demanding the same of us in our relationship with Him if we are to discover the true love He has in store for us. We cannot give something to others that we have never received. God longs to give us the love we so desperately long for and need.

Once we have allowed God to give such a love to us we are

then free to fulfill the second great command –"Love your neighbor as yourself."[2] Most couples desire to be completely accepted and appreciated for who they are. Before I was married I did an unofficial survey among various groups of singles, business people, church members, bus drivers, fast food employees, and many more. Thousands of people when asked what they look for most in someone of the opposite sex replied with something similar to 'someone who is real'. What you see is what you get. Isn't that interesting? Not money, not fame, not looks, but someone who is genuine.

Once married there are usually things we wish we didn't know. Most wives I know wish they had never been made aware of how bodily functions could be made into competitions. Most men wish they had never been made aware of many hygiene processes that are normal to women. I will NOT elaborate! Then there are the ways we are just different. I firmly believe God puts couples together as opposites in enough ways to make be real a conflict. Seriously! God makes us different so we have to learn acceptance of someone.

After getting married and having two children I discovered our sleep preferences had swapped. I became a morning person and Heather had regressed to a night person. I now found myself being completely irritated by the very practices I once adored. She sets her alarm clock an hour early and hits the snooze 13 times. That is OK unless I actually want to sleep in once in awhile. I wake at the first blast and try to figure out why anyone would want to waste uninterrupted slumber to silence a sreeking buzzer.

It is in those moments I have to remember how different we are and how God accepts me in all my imperfections. It is also a huge blessing to know my wife can see me at my worst physically, emotionally and every other way and still accepts me. That is what being real is all about. I've seen me at my worst and it is not a pretty sight. I am certain her ability to love me then comes directly from her being empowered by God. If you doubt this just give me a call and I will send you a picture of me first thing in the morning. You will quickly agree if She loves me at those moments... there is a God, He does accept anyone and has empowered my wife supernaturally to accept me. Do you get the picture? People are very different.

Now think of all the other variables involved. Different interest, skills, gifts, talents, personalities, temperaments, and the list goes on and on. Then add in God's greatest prompt for humor: Men and Women. It may have gone something like this, "I need a good laugh this millennium," God said. "I have a great idea; I'll make them male and female!"

The rest is history. Men and women start out different and become even more unique. My wife teaches middle school and loves it. I have visited her school a few times and other then the clothing styles, little has changed. Lunch time was and still is my favorite for observing male and female differences. See if you remember.

Boys finish their meal and take a piece of paper. Each folds it up into a triangle that is a what? ...A football, right! (As young men we could sit for hours grunting back and forth) "Uh, uh, uh, yah... Touchdown!!" Then they place the fingers into the shape of a miniature goal post and have a friend flick a tri-pointed object at another's face. This ritual has been repeated for generations all over the country.

The only thing more popular than football is what girls do with the same piece of paper at the same time. Their paper folding creation is much more involved and carries meaning that is vital to life as we know it. Girls spend ten times longer making their origami love connection tools.

After completion they converge and converse. Placing four fingers into this paper computer, they predict the rest of your life. A carefully selected number is given, then the shoe size, eye color, and favorite color are told to the group. Then cautiously they open a section of the paper and proclaim with great confidence, "Okay, you are going to live in the suburbs, marry Fred, have two kids, a ranch style house, drive a Volvo, and have a dog named Binky." All from this paper thing. The differences between men and women continue to grow with time.

How are you different? What makes you tick? Take a minute and get honest with God. Thank God for the things you like about one another.

Now get a little individual. Make a list of the talents you feel God has given you. Have some fun; list the personality traits you think you possess. What is your best quality? What do you think is your spouse's best quality? What does your spouse do better than anyone you know? Now list the things you wish were different. If they need to be confessed as past failures, do so.

One of my absolute favorite characteristics of God is His ability to forgive and forget. He chooses to forgive, so you and I can too. Being honest is taking the good and bad and putting it all at His feet. Once we have done that we can be free to be all He intended us to be, free to perform the ultimate gift of love. The final element of the definition. **Love is a complete commitment to getting real**, but there is one more vital element.

[1]Matthew 19:14
[2]Matthew 22:39

RECONNECTING

Discussion / Action
(approximate time 10 - 15 minutes)

1. List the two or three ways you and your spouse are most different.
2. Tell your spouse something about her/him that is different from yourself that you really appreciate?
3. Try and guess what pet peeve your spouse would love for you to give up for an entire week. Stop at 3 or 4 or when he/she agrees.
4. After two or three guesses have your spouse pick one, and commit to letting it go for 7 days.
5. Now write down which area you appreciated most about your spouse. Commit to doing something to encourage that in her/him this week. Be specific and write it down.

CHAPTER THREE

I Just Wanted To Be With You

Giving Unconditionally

I was in the final phase of my dating life with Heather (now my wife). We were at a couple's house who have been married for ten years and are still going strong. They asked the often awkward question, "So how are you two doing?" They were not asking about our general well being, rather the tone had a 'How serious are you two?' quality. It wasn't an uncomfortable question because we had talked recently and we agreed that marriage was in our future.

With this in mind, I asked our married friends to explain why we should get married. My friend Stan replied, "Well if you can't figure out the first reason you may have the gift of singleness."

I shared with great confidence that I did not have that gift. When I asked for other reasons to embark on such a committed life, to my surprise he came up with the most insightful element I had ever heard.

I began to see marriage in a whole new light. His answer has continued to give me hope and direction in how I can and should be treating my wife. It is like a light came on and I said, "Yeah, that's why marriage is set up this way. That's why complete commitment is important. That's why God thought of this in the first place." Do you want to know what he said?

Stan said, "If you are looking for someone to meet your needs, make you happy, and make your life worthwhile, you will be greatly disappointed, quickly discouraged, and basically unhappy the rest of your life. But, if you will just be the person God has made you to be, and find out how you can give your life to someone else by meeting her needs and making her happy, you will discover fulfillment, joy, and peace in ways you can't even imagine."

WOW! It made sense. The next morning I had a great time with the Lord during my Bible reflections and ended up studying what is probably the most popular verse in modern times. It was the ninth word of John 3:16. I couldn't get out of my head. *"For God so loved the world that He **gave** his only Son..."* (Emphasis added). Love is certainly a complete commitment. Love is definitely getting real with God and others. This element of giving just brings it all together. God so loved, He gave.

Success in life is not in what we get, it is in what we give. Things we obtain, power we possess, fame we achieve will never fill that lasting need we can only find in giving. Those things are temporary and there will always seem to be a need for more. When we receive something, the pleasure is for the moment and then gone forever. Giving has the opposite effect. Jesus said in Acts 20:35, "It is more blessed to give than to receive." Why?

Actually, I am not sure why, but I am discovering this is a definite fundamental truth. My greatest joys in life can be traced to times of giving. Seldom does notoriety or an object even come close to truly fulfilling our needs. It is when God chooses to use a mere human to touch a heart or meet a need that a true, lasting abundant life is discovered.

Once we allow God to give us His provision for sin, His plan for life, and His power to live it, we cannot help but want to give it away. However, we must have something to give. Understanding His complete love is paramount. The only condition to His love is our acceptance. It truly is a gift waiting for you and me to open and experience fully. I have believed this truth since inviting Christ into my heart, but not until a few years ago did God paint such a vivid picture to me of His love for us.

Fall in the Tennessee mountains was breathtaking. The leaves were brilliant; the Pigeon River deep and roaring. I sat on a rock that jutted out over the water. Dangling my feet over the edge, I reviewed my notes for the college student retreat that day. Most of all I was soaking in the colors and the crisp mountain air.

Then out of the corner of my eye something caught my attention. Walking dangerously close to the edge of the water was a little girl. She could not have been more than about four years old, and she was alone. Afraid she was going to slip off the bank and be swept away by the rushing water, I quickly got up and motioned her away from the water.

I approached the little adventurer and said, "Hi, what's your name? She quickly shot back, "What's your name?" ignoring my question. I responded, "Well, I'm Kenn. What are you doing down here?"She quizzed, "What are you doing down here?" in her new-found pattern of responses.

To avoid having to answer yet another of my own questions,

I decided to try a new approach. "I'm skipping rocks! Would you like to try?"

She didn't utter a word, but following a bold affirmative nod we were skipping rocks. While throwing I prodded for some general information. "Are your parents here? Do they know you are down here? Are they up in the cabin?"

This cute little face, focused on the new discipline of making the rocks hop, shook up and down with intermittent yet affirming grunts. I was able to decipher that her parents were indeed in the cabin above but probably did not know where she was. I suggested we skip a few more rocks then go let her parents know where we were. This seemed acceptable, and we were soon on the path up to the cabin.

It turned out that she was the associate pastor's youngest daughter, Tommi. She was four years old and had curly, bleached blonde hair, brown eyes, and loads of energy. That little bit of time she and I spent together made more of an impact on both of us than I had realized.

The day at the retreat went well, and all the sessions had gone successfully. That night would leave an indelible mark on my heart. After the final group time, I found a couch in the great room of the cabin where I was staying. The students were mingling as the fire roared. The night was cool, and a productive fatigue was quickly overtaking me.

A group of students in front of me began to part. I noticed it was Tommi making her way through the crowd. She cleared through the students and walked over to the couch where I was sitting. Without a greeting she calmly climbed up on the sofa, sat right next to me, scooted over to my hip, and nuzzled her shoulder under my outstretched arm. (Now, females did not normally approach me in this way.) Shocked and flattered, I greeted my new friend and asked, "Hi, what do you want?"

She stared at me with those big brown eyes and with a coy smile said in a shy voice, "I just wanted to be with you." Words cannot describe what happened to my heart. Where it came from I do not know. I was overcome with a flood of emotion and the sudden urge to give her my wallet, and my keys, and my money. I was thinking, "Here take it all, whatever you want."

The next day while driving to Nashville, I could not get this feeling out of my mind. I hate to use the word feeling because it was so much more than that. I prayed, "God, I am going to make the worst father in the world. She wasn't even my little girl. All she did was sit with me and I was ready to give her everything."

God has never spoken to me audibly, but this small voice in my heart was unmistakable. God moved on my heart and said, "Kenn you're going to be okay. I just wanted you to know how I feel about you every day." I will never forget that sense of complete acceptance. God longs only to give us all that is good. His love is contagious. When we truly understand it we will never be the same. We must give it away.

RECONNECTING

Discussion / Action
(approximate time 10 minutes)

1. What is something your spouse gave you during your courtship that you remember? How did it make you feel? Why?

2. What does your spouse give to you that makes you feel the most loved:
    A) Focused time together
    B) Gifts, cards, or other items
    C) Physical closeness (not just sex, but touching; hugs, kisses, etc.)
    D) Service: completes tasks, helps around the house,
    E) Kind words of reassurance (spoken, written, overheard, etc.)[1]

3. Remind your spouse of a time in the past few months (the more recent the better) when he/she gave the type love you most enjoy.

4. This week make a specific effort to show the type love your spouse enjoys most.

[1] Gary Chapman <u>Five Love Languages</u>

CHAPTER FOUR

Big Macs And Vitamins

Fundamental vs. Supplemental Intimacy Needs

*S*ixth grade was a confusing and exciting time. Changing classes for the first time, getting a locker, wearing cool clothes (well, we thought they were cool at the time), and discovering that girls were no longer gross. Sixth grade was my first real encounter with love. Looking back from any point in life, the previous stage always seems easier doesn't it? Junior high certainly seemed easy for me as I think back. I doubt the standard procedure has changed much since the invention of the writing utensil.

Three weeks into the first quarter I received my first love note. Prompted by one cute sixth grader, but written and delivered by her best friend. The note read something like:

Kenny,
Neia likes you. Do you like her?
YES or No
(Circle one)

Girls knew they needed to write out, "Circle one" or the guy would stand there for hours trying to figure out what to do next. Love sure was simple then. I circled my response, and before I knew it, we were going together. I am not sure where we went, but for three glorious days we went together. We swapped name bracelets and it was the most…different time of my life. I must not have gone together correctly or something because I soon received another note saying Neia did not want to go with me anymore. Oh, yes, and to give back her bracelet.

I still have the problem of trying to figure out what exactly the woman in my life wants. I often wish there were a note with simple options and a "circle one" feature. Marriage is a bit more complicated, but that same desire to be with my special someone remains. I have a genuine desire to be married. I love being married. Yet, there are those times where it just doesn't click. I have the ability to completely frustrate the precious, gracious woman that pledged her life to me. I have never awoken and thought, "Today I want to thoroughly tick off my wife. I hope to make her world miserable and completely disappoint her." While I have never set out with this goal I have accomplished it on several occasions. How can I minimize these times for both of our sakes? How does this relate to the desire I have for her and both our needs for one another?

FUNDAMENTAL INTIMACY SOURCE

God designed us with a natural need for intimacy. The problem is that we do not take the time to find the right intimacy to meet the right need. Most failure and frustration comes from a misunderstanding about the types of and the need for intimacy. As Bill Hybles in his book, *Fit To Be Tied*, puts it so beautifully, "Perhaps we fail to understand that God created human beings to yearn for **two levels of relational intimacy**. The first level can be met by establishing a deep, honest, trusting relationship with a friend or marriage partner. The second level can only be met by entering into an authentic, growing relationship with God."[1] (Emphasis added.)

The most important or fundamental intimacy need we have has very little, if anything, to do with our spouse. Jesus did not say in John 10:10, "I came that they may have life and have it abundantly..."[2] Once they get married The abundant life, (hope, peace, joy, fulfillment, happiness), is contingent on only one type of intimacy. Fundamental intimacy. People have tried throughout time to fill this fundamental need with supplemental sources and it never works.

Money, power, marriage, sex, drugs, fame... nothing can fill the fundamental need for intimacy except the fundamental source. That fundamental source is a personal relationship with God.

The fundamental intimacy I am trying to communicate is the deep desire for significance. That need for everything to be OK. The craving we have to be know as special unique person we always felt we were. It may be the longing to know that the past is healed or the pain won't return. Whatever the form in your life it is a fundamental need we all have in some specifically unique form. God created us this way so we would have a longing to for that fundamental relationship with Him. The problems all couples have in varying degrees is dues to the efforts of expecting their spouse to meet this God sized intimacy need. God is the only one who can meet those needs and satisfy those cravings. Although God has done all the work to provide the opportunity for a relationship, it is clear we as individuals make that choice to start and establish the relationship. In Rev. 3:20, Jesus says to you and me, "Behold, I stand at the door and knock. If any one hears my voice and opens the door I will come in..."

Several pastors have made the observation that the only door knob is on the inside, and only we can open that door. Finding the source to meet our fundamental intimacy need is as easy as opening that door. The process is laid out for whosoever, anybody (John 3:16). When we agree with God that we have sinned and fall short of being perfect, (Romans 3:23), we have taken the first step. When we accept that Jesus took the punishment for that sin and imperfection (Romans 6:23) we have taken the second step. The decisive step, though, is when we of our own will choose to believe that Jesus is the only forgiveness for our sin (John 14:6) and that we place our hope and trust in Him. We invite Him into our lives to forgive our imperfections and direct our lives. (1 John 5:11-13). The fundamental intimacy source begins to fill the fundamental intimacy need. Yes, I said begins to fill.

Are we complete in Christ when we invite Him into our lives? YES! Yet, we must establish this source as our fundamental supply. Too many Christians (me included) for too long have the complete, perfect **fundamental** source yet keep looking to **supplemental** supplies to meet this need.

Let's move from the theoretical into hard reality. There is an over-whelming attitude among many Christians today of, "Once I invite Christ into my life, I can do things the way I think or feel they should be done, pray about them, and God should bless me." It would be like me as a child saying to my earthly father, "I accept the fact that you are my Dad. I will now do things my way and you should bless me." My way was often greeted with the blessing of a spanking, discipline, and time in my room to ponder who was in control. Our heavenly Father is infinitely wise and He knows what is going to meet our needs.

Prayer is not a vending machine nor is God a brainless genie. The way we experience God meeting our fundamental needs, providing peace, directing us to hope, and finding us the path to fulfillment is by individually establishing that fundamental supply. In plain English, doing it His way or not at all.

For too long I had thought that since I am a Christian and God is forgiving, loving, and gracious that I could do what I thought was right and He would bless or forgive my actions and everything just worked out, right? God is gracious, loving, and understanding and does... "work all thing together for our good..." (Romans 8:28) But don't miss the end of this verse, "... to those who love God and are called according to His purpose."

We must allow God to provide the fundamental intimacy in our lives and direct us according to His plan. The way we do this is by committing in our hearts to pursue relationships according to His purpose or not at all. We will not always understand His way, yet we must choose to follow it. His way will not always feel natural, but we must choose His way anyway. It may not be the popular way, but we must choose to trust it.

As dedicated sons and daughters, we must stop sprinkling religious words and deeds on our self conceived ideas expecting them to meet our fundamental intimacy needs. Another major fault I am guilty of is expecting his blessing on my relationships due to obedience to His will in other areas of my life. This attitude is wrong. As Galatians 6:7 simply states, whatever we sow, we will reap. Therefore, we must plant the right seeds in every area of our lives. We have to ask ourselves, are we the best husband, the best father, the type friend, the type employee or golfer that God wants us to be? I threw the golfer thing in there for my sake (you fill in the blanks for your life).

If we are not experiencing the fundamental intimacy need being met in our lives, then we either don't have the proper relationship with God, or we are not trusting His way it in the relationship area of our lives. Establishing the trust in Him as the fundamental source is vital to our relational success.

Even at the ripe old age of seven I wanted to be successful in everything I did. At that age football was much more important to me than relationships, though. When I look back it is clear the faithfulness of God was there to teach me this truth even then.

The Smyrna Jets needed a linebacker, and this sixty-five pound boy was it. The pads were bigger than I was, but at that age it was so cool to wear the uniform and act like the big guys. Football was not big in our family yet my Dad was still very supportive. Each week he would sit up on the grassy bank next to the field and watch the games. On the way home from each game we would talk about many issues related to football but mostly about how I played. Two games in particular stick out in my mind from that year.

One week in the middle of the season we had won big. Four touchdowns! After the game I could not wait to hear my dad's reaction to the skill and effort of the outside linebacker more commonly know as Kenny. We rehashed the game and the five or six tackles I made. As we drove into the neighborhood my Dad made a closing comment that stuck with me. "You played a great game, but do you remember the play in the last quarter when you were winning by five touchdowns? The one where they ran a reverse with two and a half minutes left?"

I shrugged it off with a, "Yeah, he was gone by a mile and we were going to win anyway. It didn't matter."

"Yeah, it does matter," my Dad gently but firmly injected. "You never know what can happen. He could have stumbled, or fallen, or fumbled, and you need to be there to make every play you can. **You never give up**. They could have scored and gotten a couple on-side kicks." At that age I believed everything my Dad said, and in Pee-Wee football anything can happen. "Play until you hear the whistle. Never give up. You played a good game."

I did not think another thing about it. I recounted my great plays to my Mom and was bigger than life for a week. The next week was not so great. Instead of leading by five touchdowns, we were losing by four touchdowns, down 24 points (little guys don't often make extra points). Worse, it was raining and it was about forty degrees. This was not fun.

With less than a minute left, the other team ran a sweep to the opposite side and my team was not too intent on stopping them. What did it matter? Lose by 24 points or 30, who cares? Their tail back was twenty yards ahead of everyone. Then this voice in my helmet started going off. Play till the whistle, NEVER GIVE UP! I took off with the ultimate of optimism. I'll catch him, he'll fumble, I'll run it back, touchdown, on-side kick, we could still win..."

As the rain beat down and the cold gripped me, I realized everyone else on the field quit running except the guy with the ball and me.

As we trounced trough the puddles and mud, he slowed up a little. I closed the gap from fifteen yards, to ten yards, to five yards, his jersey was right at my fingertips...

Now, this would be a great story... if I had caught the guy. If he had fumbled and I had the chance to score it would have been such a wonderful example. He did not fumble. All I caught was a cold. I was wet and cold, and now exhausted. The final horn sounded and we lost by five touchdowns. Frustrated, wet, dejected, and a little mad, I made my way up the grassy hill, took off my shoulder pads, soaked and muddy, I climbed into our Plymouth Valiant, my chin on my chest and my lower lip puffed out.

Dad got into the car. Without pausing he said, "You played a great game!"

Wondering if he had watched my game, I said, " What?" I didn't lift my head and I was about to cry from embarrassment.

"That last play," he said.

In a minor fit of anger I said with my head buried, "He didn't fumble, I didn't catch him, and we lost!"

"That doesn't matter," he said with a proud grin. "He scored but you didn't give up! I was so proud of you!"

For the first time I looked out the window and I noticed we weren't going home. Where are we going? McDonalds! (I lit up like a Christmas tree.) When we arrived the surprise got even better. My Dad, who was very tight with money, shocked me. My sister, brother and I never got to order anything but what kind of drink we wanted. It was always a small hamburger, small fries, then we could pick a small Coke or Sprite.

But, not this trip. The young lady asked for our order. My dad turned to me and said, "Go ahead." In shock I asked him what he meant. He said, "Anything you want." Wow! I could get a Big Mac, no, I want two Big Macs, large fry, large Coke, large chocolate milk shake. Seven years old and sixty-five pounds – I sat there with a Big Mac in each hand.

The game long forgotten and all I could think about was, "I DIDN'T GIVE UP! No one will likely ever remember that the Vikings beat the Jets in Smyrna that day, but I learned something that I will never forget.

God longs to teach us in the same way. Our relationships can be unforgettably great when we choose to establish God and His way as the fundamental source for all our needs. We must commit to having relationships with our spouses His way or our marriages cannot be what they were created to be.

SUPPLEMENTAL INTIMACY SOURCE

I love my wife Heather more than golf. I love her more than Ben & Jerry's Chocolate Chip Cookie Dough Ice Cream. I love my wife more than breathing. I love her more than food. Okay, you get the idea. As much as I love her and would do anything for her, I cannot now nor will I ever be able to compete with God. He is just too awesome. He can use absolutes you and I can only talk about. He can say things like "...surely I am with you *always*..." (Matthew 28:20) and, "***Never*** will leave you…" (Hebrews 13:5).[1] He can back up each statement. How can we compete with that?

You may be saying to that absurd question, "Kenn you have lost it; of course we cannot compete with that." But, how many of us try? How many of us expect another human to meet the fundamental needs only God can? Numerous relationships and marriages tragically fail for this very reason. A wife looks for her husband to meet her fundamental need for security. A husband looks for his wife to meet his fundamental need for significance. These are pressures to meet a need that God and God alone can satisfy. It is only when we realize that another person cannot and will not make us totally happy, bring us complete joy, provide us with lasting peace, and give constant fulfill-ment that we begin to discover marriage the way God created it.

From the very beginning we see that God designed men and women to be a supplemental intimacy source to meet supplemental intimacy needs. In Genesis chapter two we find Adam rooting around the garden. He is making it happen. He is naming animals, growing food, digging a garden within the garden.

Imagine Adam on his knees trenching trough the dirt with a rock. Dig, dig, grunt, grunt. The garden is happening and is fundamentally fine. Then comes verse 18 and God says, "It is not good for the man to be alone, I will make him a helper..." God was probably thinking, "Hey, Adam is going to ignore the directions or go walking and get lost. Look, he is digging with a rock..."

Enter the helper suitable for him. Eve quietly stands next to Adam and says, "Here, try this shovel!" Adam grabs it and starts digging away with much more success.

Notice that our friend Adam was getting it done. All the fundamental needs met. Eve came along to simply make it better. But, if we look to that supplemental source to meet our fundamental needs, look out. Adam knew the source for all his needs. When he listened to the supplemental source, Eve, to meet a fundamental need, Wisdom and Knowledge, there was trouble. Adam is thinking the shovel was a good idea. Why not trust the helper God gave me instead of God? Have an apple? Okay. Wrong!

A supplemental source was never meant to meet a fundamental need. It is important in relationships to never put the expectations and pressures on anyone to meet our fundamental needs. The relationship can only result in failure. Supplemental vitamins are good if they are taken in conjunction with a well balanced diet. It does not matter how great the vitamins are if there is no food in the diet.

Allow me to paint a very clear picture of how this truth should look in the reality of relationships. Philippians 4:4-5 says "Rejoice in the Lord always, again: Rejoice! Let your gentle spirit be known to men the Lord is near."[3] We should be so fundamentally 'full' that we can walk into every type of social situation this way. Happiness is the result because we do not need anything—we already have it all.

No one can make us happy. We are already happy. You cannot bring someone complete peace when he or she already has it. Joy? Already got it. Purpose? Got it. The only things not brought to the party are an unrealistic agenda and expectations. You cannot lose with this person. He expects nothing from you, so anything is a bonus for you. The best anyone can do is help you and me be more of what we already are. God has met all our needs. Phillipians 4:6 says that if I do have any needs to take them to the fundamental source, and He will take care of them.

The greatest part of understanding this truth is in Phil. 4:7. When we trust Him to meet our fundamental needs, He makes us a promise that anyone who has ever been disappointed or broken-hearted can hold on to. Trust Him and He will give you and me peace that surpasses comprehension, that will guard our hearts and minds. We won't get hurt or carry unrealistic expectations. Believe me, it works and if you want to avoid making the same mistakes over and over, establish God as your source to meet your fundamental needs. His peace and protection are worth it.

RECONNECTING

Discussion / Action
(approximate time 10 minutes)

1. What is your spouses favorite:
    Meal:
    Beverage:
    Color:
    Vacation Spot:

2. Describe to your spouse what an intimate evening out would look like.

3. Together discuss the difference between Fundamental and Supplemental intimacy.

4. Describe to your spouse where you are on your spiritual journey. If you have a relationship with Christ share when, where, or how that happened.

[1]Hybels, Bill. *Fit To Be Tied*
(Grand Rapids, MI: Zondervan Pub. House, 1991), p.32.
[2]New American Standard (Here after referred to NAS)
(Chicago, IL. Moody Press, 1995)
[3]NAS

SECTION TWO

RECONNECTING OUR
Attitudes

*M*en read in the bathroom. Married men read in th bathroom more than single men. Married fathers read in the bathroom as if it were a lounge chair on the beach. I am not sure where the tradition started but I feel the need to continue the idea. The only negative experience I ever had originated from my in-laws guest bedroom. It was a mental not physical problem. Do not be afraid. This does not get gross. While Heather and I were dating we took several trips to her parents home a state away. They had a beautiful home. Her father is a successful executive and her mother an interior decorator.

While the guest bathroom was certainly decorated beautifully there was not much to read. There was a basket full of magazines in the appropriate place but they were all decorating magazines. After a few trips I broke down and started reading the home beautifying material. I read the toothpaste, shaving crÉme, and shampoo bottle until I had memorized them. The problem came when I realized how those times had effected me.

Returning from a weekend away with the in-laws I found myself in the home of a friend who had not married. He had a great guy's home. BIG screen TV just off the kitchen. This is all the decorating a man really needs. I was there to watch the game and enjoy some male bonding. The conversations bantered about the room discussing the weekend's college games as we awaited the Monday night football game. As the conversation came around to me I had one real thought on my mind that I almost said out loud, "You know this room would look great with a boarder and a chair rail." Lucky for me I did not say it! The guys asked if I was about to say anything and I quietly declined. Why was that on the tip of my tongue? Because that is what I had put into my brain for several trips. That is what was freshest on my mind.

When our attitudes are primed with the foundation of what is really best for our marriages that too will be on the forefront of our minds. That is what this section is all about. What are you focused on with regard to how your marriage should be? What truth have you been dwelling on in order to refine your attitude around the house? What principle has penetrated your mind to effect your actions to better serve your spouse? Lets invest in a few truths that can radically alter our attitude and revolutionize our marriages.

CHAPTER FIVE

Lasting Love Absolutely Guaranteed

Secrets of Love:
Expect Nothing & Appreciate Everything

*L*ittle Chad was a shy, quiet young man. One day he came home and told his mother that he'd like to make a valentine for everyone in his class. Her heart sank. She thought, "I wish he wouldn't do that!" She had watched the children when they walked home from school. Her Chad was always behind them. They laughed and hung on to each other and talked to each other, but Chad was never included. Nevertheless, she decided she would go along with her son. So she purchased the paper and glue and crayons. For three weeks, night after night, Chad painstakingly made 35 valentines.

Valentine's Day dawned, and Chad was beside himself with excitement. He carefully stacked them up, put them in a bag, and bolted out the door. His mother decided to bake him his favorite cookies and serve them nice and warm with a cool glass of milk when he came home from school. She just knew he would be disappointed and maybe that would ease the pain a little. It hurt her to think that he wouldn't get many valentines-maybe none at all.

That afternoon she had the cookies and milk on the table. When she heard the children outside, she looked out the window. Sure enough, there they came, laughing and having the best time. And, as always, there was Chad in the rear. He walked a little faster than usual. She fully expected him to burst into tears as soon as he got inside. His arms were empty, she noticed, and when the door opened she choked back the tears.

"Mommy has some cookies and milk for you," she said.

But he hardly heard her words. He just marched right on by, his face aglow, and all he could say was: "Not a one. Not a one."

Her heart sank.

And then he added, "I didn't forget a one, not a single one!"[1]

Proper attitude when approaching love is vital. To be in love we must first become love ourselves (as defined in Chapter 8). One important way to accomplish this is with one of the most important attitude correcting statements in all of scripture located in Philippians 2:3 *"Do nothing from selfishness or empty conceit..."*

We will be hard pressed to find anyone who genuinely wants a loving marriage and boldly proclaims him or herself conceited or selfish. The difficult part is when we honestly evaluate our lives and allow God to reveal the areas that are selfish and empty. Even more difficult is the process of allowing the needed changes to take place. When God began to work on the selfishness and conceit in my life, I clearly saw the depth of the problem.

I considered myself the last person on the earth who could be deemed selfish, but I later discovered selfishness had been often disguised as good intentions.

Philippians 2:3 came across my devotion time. Praying for meaning in my life, I discovered my attitude of selfishness. I was giving wholeheartedly, ten-fold, hoping and expecting only to get a little something in return. That was the mistake; I was giving to get. Even expecting a small return, giving to get is selfish and does not accomplish God's will. It is a wrong attitude.

Another wrong attitude that seems so natural is that of conceit. None of us wants to be thought of as conceited. "My best quality is my conceit." The heart of conceit is when we stop improving on the areas we know need work, and instead evaluate others by our expectations. We judge ourselves by our ideals and others by their actions. It is so innocent, yet so natural to focus outwardly.

Let's get personal for a minute. If I were to ask you 2 or 3 ways your spouse needed improvement could you identify them? If I were to ask you how he or she frustrated you in the past 48 hours would you be able to think of a few ways? Now, take a minute and do some self-evaluation. Be honest for a minute. We will start easy. Do you have any weaknesses in your life at all? I told you we would start easy. Do you have any flaws that are a frustration to your spouse? Now comes the killer. What did you proactively, purposefully, intentionally do today to get better in any area in which you need work?

Better yet, which is easier to identify the shortcomings of your spouse or the actions needed to improve yourself? Part of being human is the ability to see our strengths while often choosing to be blind to our weaknesses. It is also very natural to passively notice our spouse's faults before actively considering how to improve ourselves.

We will not embody godly qualities by evaluating others. Always remember that God works from the inside out. Our happiness does not hinge on how picky we can be with someone else. The successes of our relationships are determined by how well we embody the qualities and attitudes of love. Well, you may ask, if selfishness and empty conceit are the wrong attitudes, what are the correct attitudes? This is a great question answered in Philippians 2:3-4.

EXPECT NOTHING

"But with humility of mind..." [2] (Philippians 2:3) What is humility of mind? It is not a degrading of ourselves. Humility is not saying, we are nothing, worse than a worm, no, worse than a worm in a well, no worse than a worm in a dry well in the cracks of the dirt, you get the picture. Humility is having a proper perspective with regard to our Heavenly Father. We may consciously or unconsciously think, "Why didn't God give me the marriage I dreamed of? I did everything right." Or wish God would just fix my spouse in a way that will make my life what I always thought it should be.

After a long look at this, I realized my understanding of and attitude towards humility were all wrong. God has already done it all. Why am I asking the God, who controls it all, why He is not changing to meet my needs? My attitude must change to ask in humility of mind, "God how do you want me to change in order to experience what you have already planned?"

We must come to realize God owes us nothing! He has lived the perfect example of love for us, taken all our faults and failure, and died for them so we could be free. Upon request He lives within us to guide and direct us when we are willing to listen. He owes us nothing. He has given us everything, and in our foolishness we ask for something He has already provided.

If we desire a perfect marriage, we must seek Him with all of our hearts and seek to become all He is. We must shift to a non-expectant attitude that humbly says, "God if You never did another thing for me, You have done enough." At that point we will begin to have the scales fall from our eyes and see the love He has already provided.

I heard from a well-meaning Christian wife who believed she married the wrong man and felt she would never be happy. What a sad attitude! Not to over simplify things, but the problem in this woman's life is most likely not the wrong man, but her wrong attitude. She is obviously expecting this man to be something or do something which she has decided he is incapable of accomplishing. She lacks a key attitude. Expecting Nothing. This includes dying to self. Look at the progression Jesus took in Philippians 2:5-9.

Humble, Servant, Obedient
Death, Cross, God Exalted

If we are going to have a successful marriage and have edifying relationships, we must learn the attitude of dying to one's self. This phrase appears often in the Christian walk, and only recently have I understood its meaning. I thought dying to self meant a complete apathy toward an area of life. None of the successful marriages that I personally know of have any form of apathy. I will just do what I am told and expect my wife/husband to be happy. Denial of our desires is not the answer. It is also a leading cause of frustration, depression, and disharmony. I have seen this attitude first hand. "I did what you wanted now leave me alone." Or, "I completed your list now I get to do my thing." Dying to self is not giving up our will, rather it is merging our will with something better and more significant.

God's plan is much better and more reasonable. Dying to self is an active pursuit of our Heavenly Father's way. Simply put, it is to ***do it God's way***. When we choose this route, we relinquish control. We trust in God to make things happen. Remember clearly in Jesus' life how he was wronged, His rights violated, His life taken, but for trust in God the Father, His created purpose was fulfilled.

Marriage is meant to be a wonderful life filling experience. God is fully aware that marriage has its moments of frustration and hard knocks. God's desire is that all that efforts does not go to waste. When we connect with His purpose, plan, and empowerment those times have meaning and ultimately bring fulfillment. Without allowing God to control our lives (humility) we do more work, with little connection and the results are momentary at best. With God running the show those same efforts have meaning and pay major benefits. Those efforts grow depth and the connection from those frustrations actually adds to the richness in the marriage.

If you doubt this concept think back to some of the first disagreements of your marriage. Chances are you look back and laugh now. They were so insignificant, yet they were huge at the time. When God is in control we grow and our connection strengthens. Those minor details gain proper priority and actually add strength and depth to our relationship. Now, to realize that desire within His perfect plan, we must die to self. Our attitude must be the one of doing it God's way or no way at all. Our expectations must turn completely inward and our lives must begin to align with His word, His will, and His way. Our expectation of others must become zero, and must focus inward to how we are becoming who God desires us to be.

Expecting Nothing is an attitude adjustment toward God and toward ourselves, but most practically toward others. We must set our attitude toward others as having no agenda and no evaluation, thus no expectations. Love is first and foremost what we give. Jesus states the attitude we must have in Luke 6:35.

"But love your enemies, and do good, and lend, __expecting nothing__ in return; and your reward will be great, and you will be sons of the Most High; for He Himself is kind to ungrateful and evil men." [3]

I know God has a sense of humor. He chose to teach me this verse in a very practical way at the very beginning of my marriage. I started learning the truths shared in this book and thought I was ready to apply them to my life. God had His agenda to teach me the attitude of expecting nothing.

Two weeks following a wonderful honeymoon we were at home on a Saturday ready to continue in our bliss of setting up our home. The tiny condo was easy enough for one person to clean, but there was a certain joy in doing it together on Saturday mornings. We are blessed to have a very similar definition of clean. I know couples range from neat freak married to a slob all the way to perfectionist married to a momma's boy. When we married I was 30 so cleaning had become a normal routine for me. Heather also kept a nice apartment before our nuptials so we thought this would be the least of our worries. For the most part it was until week three at home.

After two weeks of unofficially splitting the chores I decided to make a little change. Heather had performed a certain set of cleaning task for two weeks and I did the other half. This particular week I decided to do the chores she had done previously so as to not impose that set of duties on her. She followed my lead by tackling the duties I had previously done with one exception. While the bathroom was clean the tub had been missed. I rationalize this oversight by thinking the curtain had been pulled and she just missed it. The fact our bathroom was so small two people could not fit in it at the same time was only a minor issue. The next week I decided to see if my "tub oversight" theory was correct. I was sure to get up first and select the set of chores that left the tub on her list to do. After all was done I went to take a shower and more specifically check the tub. Once again the bathroom was spectacular except for the bathtub. I called to my precious bride and bid her presence in the oversized closet with running water. I gave glorious compliments to her cleaning ability and praised her work then sheepishly added, "But, you missed the bathtub." Standing in the doorway her facial expression and body language communicated an awareness that indicated she understood my true intention of point out the fault. Her response made it unmistakably clear that her actions were intentional and not soon to change. She was kirt and while turning and walking away said, "Oh, I don't do bathtubs!"

Everything in my body bowed up. The hair on the back of my neck stood on end. She was gone before I could counter. I stood there thinking, "You do NOW!" Before I could make it to the door so we could have our first conversational growth opportunity (formally known to couples as a fight) that "expect nothing" concept and verse came to my mind. I literally thought, "Not now God. I am going to deal with this one my way." I stopped. I took a deep breath and listened to God's still small voice. Questions came to my mind that I really did not want to hear at that moment. "Kenn, if you found this information out the day of your wedding would you have still married her? If you had to do all the tub cleaning the rest of your life would that price be worth paying for such a wonderful woman?" Then it went to an even deeper level. Who ever said it was her job and 50/50 was the rule. I should be thankful that I don't have to do everything. This is not an easy place to get to nor is it easy to live there but it sure is the right place to be.

Jesus commands us to expect nothing when He spoke of loving and giving to our enemies. It is imperative that this attitude be fundamental in the relationships with those we do want to be with. The first absolute attitude is to...***Expect Nothing!***

APPRECIATE EVERYTHING

Everyone likes to be appreciated. Genuine appreciation comes in many forms and is always welcome. Every time I open the mail box I look through the bills and junk mail hoping to find anything that is hand written. It has such a personal touch. We feel so appreciated when someone takes the time to simply write us or say hello. What a great action to signify appreciation.

The Apostle Paul writes in I Thessalonians 5:18 another absolute attitude, "In everything give thanks; for this is God's will for you in Christ Jesus." If we ever want to find God's will for a happy successful marriage we must develop an attitude of gratitude.

In some areas it is easy After thirty years of being single, and after a difficult but very worthwhile process of change, I got married. I had been conditioned while single that if it was going to get done around the house I was going to have to be the one to do it.

The first few months of marriage were unbelievable. I would come home thinking of a hundred things to get done before my next trip only to find my wife had done half of them already and even started many others. The laundry was already in the dryer, the house was dusted, bills paid, calls returned. WOW! Thank you, Thank you, Thank you! We both realized the benefit of an expect nothing attitude by doing for one another. The appreciation just followed.

A problem occurs when what once was appreciated is now

expected. We must fight with all our heart, soul and mind to never fall into the trap of forgetting how to appreciate the other person in our relationship. We must continuously set our mind and hearts on being appreciative of the basics.

Heather and I recently enjoyed a great attitude of gratitude re-set. Metro Bible Study in Atlanta has a group that has been going down town each Friday night for the past twenty years. This group is not going to the theater, a ball game, or a concert. They go to the same empty parking lot each week to meet with the homeless.

A couple of the people put the event together by rounding up food and some donated clothes. There is music, a message, and then dinner and clothes to be passed out. Mostly it is a time to give and encourage. This experience ranks as one of the richest I have personally ever been involved with. Jesus said, *"...whatever you did for one of the least of these brothers of mine you did for me."* [5] I saw Jesus up close and personal through the eyes of these homeless people.

Jesus also said, *"The poor you will always have with you..."* [6] I do not know what city you live in, but I do know there are needs in your community. This type of ministry is not for everyone, but it is a great way to focus on this principle of expecting nothing and appreciating everything. Finding a group that is involved with meeting needs is relatively easy. Making the time to invest in others lives is never wasted time. These types of projects establish a lasting memory of what it means to expect nothing and appreciate everything.

Appreciation can also erode when we begin taking others for granted. When was the last time we took the five minutes to write a note to our spouse? When was the last time we did something we were not required to for someone who really needed encouragement? Are we looking for opportunities to show appreciation or simply waiting to notice when everybody else does? Genuine appreciation takes place by choice not by reaction.

This was never more evident than when I heard an elderly couple respond to a question about marriage. Some friends were making a video for a couple who were soon to be married. Not only did they capture the comments and advice from numerous friends and family, they went one better. Toting a video camera, they went to our city square and asked total strangers to give a good luck message.

Many offered best wishes or offered advice.

The videographer later came across an elderly couple holding hands walking in the square. They approached and asked if they would be willing to take part in this endeavor. The couple agreed, and the camera rolled. The sweet couple was asked how long they had been married and if they had any advice for the couple to be. "Fifty-one years," replied the wife with a shy smile.

And what advice did they have for the soon-to-be couple? The gentleman paused, squeezed his wife's hand and said, "Oh, I don't know much about advice. I guess you just don't take each other for granted. Every week for the last fifty-one years we have had a date. It's what we are doing right now. I guess that would be it."

What an answer! Each week for the past half a century he asks his bride for a night out. For half a century she has said yes. Isn't that precious? Appreciation takes time. Appreciation takes effort.

Watching as the couple walked away holding hands smiling, it sure seemed worth it. I am certain over those fifty-one years they had learned the importance of appreciating everything. One of the key attitudes of appreciating everything is to not take anything for granted.

Appreciating the basics is important. Not taking things for granted is vital, but let's take a quantum leap and look at another key to appreciating everything. The writer of Hebrews states it very well in verse 10:24, "let us consider how to stimulate one another to love and good deeds."[7] One of the greatest ways to appreciate is to stimulate. There, it even rhymes.

What stimulates your spouse. Is it time away to focus, is it little gifts that say you were thinking about her. Is it a note in his briefcase that says you are proud of him. How about surprising her with a maid and a note that says how much you appreciate her efforts all year so take this one off. All it takes is a little thought and effort. I guarantee you will not regret it and your spouse will not forget it!

Certainly use this idea in your marriage but export it as well.

As I continue to learn this attitude of gratitude, the opportunities seem to be everywhere; I just have to take the time to look. My wife and I were on our way to church and turned on the radio. We found a station playing some really upbeat non-liturgical Christian music. A lot of the best tunes with some great beat. Heather wondered what station was playing. We looked down to see that it was one of the major secular stations in our city. They had set aside some time on Sunday morning to play the most upbeat Christian stuff they could find. It may not be for everyone, but we sure liked it.

We talked about taping the show so we could enjoy it during the week. Heather said, "We need to write them a tell them this is great." My first thought was that they already knew, but she was right. Here was a station taking a chance, and it really encouraged us. I began to think of the other areas of life I had been encouraged and almost immediately someone came to mind. James Cook.

James is a custodian at a local Junior High school. He is also one of the most faithful prayer warriors I know. Each week at the Metro Bible Study he volunteers to take all the prayer requests and prays over each one. After they are shared with the group they are handed over to James. Of the hundreds of people attending, there may be a handful that know about James.

God prompted my heart with, "You know about him; do something." It was a simple note that took maybe five minutes to write. It is important that he knew someone appreciated his faithful efforts and that he was encouraged to continue what he was doing. Who is the James in your life? We see them every day. Whose day can you make a little brighter? If we develop this attitude with those in our everyday life it is more likely to be second nature at home.

A big key to appreciation is initiation. Appreciation is most often communicated by simple effort. Take what is common, add some effort, and what do you get? Something special. Some friends of mine in the past were masters at this.

One time they had the idea of going to dinner and a movie. Pretty common right? Here is the kicker. These guys invited me to get involved in the planning. We decided on a group date. There was a movie coming out that everyone wanted to see. We added some extra effort and abracadabra...special.

The men went to the fast food restaurant selling the commemorative plastic cups for the movie we wanted to see. After collecting several cups, we planned a picnic for the evening at a local park. The guys gave the ladies an invitation that said when to meet us and where (map included). Upon their arrival we enjoyed a picnic dinner together and the question eventually came up, "What movie are we going to see?"

We answered, "Look at your cups!" They wanted to see that movie, but knew it was sold out that particular weekend. (But not if you had a friend stand in line at 4:00pm for tickets.) They were so surprised at how we got the tickets. This may sound corny, but you would not believe the mileage we got from that evening.

We would have seen the movie anyway, but we decided to take a little time and add some effort for it to become a night to remember. It was funny to be at parties after months had passed and one of those cups would show up. Without fail the story was told by an appreciative participant. All the ladies were very impressed with our creativity.

Appreciation takes time. Appreciation takes effort. But, to see a face light up, and a heart filled with joy make it certainly worth the effort. How does God desire to develop an attitude of gratitude in you? Are we thanking God for the basics of life afforded us today? Who are the people in our influence that could benefit from a word of appreciation? Are we taking spouses for granted? Have we considered how to stimulate him/her to love and to do good deeds today? Take something common in your week; add some effort and see how special God can make you in someone's life.

Write down in the space below your spouses name and two other people you appreciate. Now write down three to five ways to show appreciation. Match an expression of appreciation with each person. Try not to do the same for each in order to practice variety. Write down the date of a realistic deadline, and go for it.

Draw a box next to each person's name and when the effort is put forth, put a check in the box. This exercise may be easier or more difficult than you think. The important part is to **do it**. Through your efforts God will begin to mold in you an attitude of gratitude not to mention make someone's day very special.

RECONNECTING

Discussion / Action

1. What is your spouse's favorite treat
   (Candy, espresso, cake, etc.)?

2. Identify an item you have recently purchased that
   disappointed you or did not live up to expectations.

3. Name something your spouse did in the past week
   that you appreciate.

4. Name 5 things you are thankful for as a couple.

5. Which absolute (Expect Nothing <> Appreciate Everything)
   is most natural to you?

[1]Galloway, Dale. *A 3rd Serving of Chicken Soup For The Soul*.
(Deerfield Beach, FL. Health Communications, Inc. 1996)
[2]NAS
[3]NAS (Emphasis added)
[4]NAS
[5]Matt. 25:40
[6]Matt. 26:11
[7]NAS

CHAPTER SIX

Road Map To Love

Defining And Becoming The Character Of Love

/

*D*ream big. In Psalms 37:4 we see that if we delight in the Lord He will give us the desires of our hearts. Ephesians 3:20 states that God is able to do more than we can ask for or dream. What ever happened to the idea that dreams come true? It certainly was not God's idea to quit dreaming. Too many think that the handsome, nurturing, romantic man or the beautiful, smart, supportive woman will have to exist only in fantasy or memories.

Our dreams have been replaced with the harsh reality of compromise, failure, routine, busyness and fatigue. What occurs many times is that reality of the past pushes our dreams into a room marked unrealistic wishes. Good news: God is in the business of cleaning out rooms and making dreams a reality again.

The question is are you ready? A problem married folks, is that we are looking to find that dream instead of becoming that very love we are looking for. Instead of passively sitting back and hoping fate will smile upon us and that special someone will change or understand. God has a much better idea. It is time we quit asking the question, "Why aren't you like you used to be?" and started asking, "**How have I changed? How do I need to change?**"

Contrary to popular belief God has a lot to say about finding that specific love we are searching for. He has a well detailed plan with some very detailed directions. It is our choice to take Him at His word and start moving toward the goal. We have to take the plan, follow the directions and start becoming the love we desire.

THE PLAN

The starting point of the PLAN is the same for everyone. Only God could come up with a plan that works no matter what your situation. If you are a newlywed wanting to make the best foundation possible it works. If you have been married for 50 years and wish you had some of those sparks from the past it is exactly what you need. If you have a great marriage and want to shine the glow or if you just cannot get on the same page it will guide you to the desired destination.

Before we look at the plan specifically I want to give a bit of guidance. Look at this plan in three different lights. How intently you look at these different questions will depend on where you are in the relationship spectrum.

1) Ask, do *I* embody the qualities of this plan?

2) Does *the person* I am devoted to strive to embody these qualities?

3) Is *our* marriage completely committed to these qualities?

I have seen many times two wonderful people follow the plan on their own and ruin a great relationship by not following the plan together.

So, what is this plan?

The plan is found in Philippians 4:8-9. But before it is revealed let me make one last endorsement. Without exception, every time I have been frustrated or been at odds with my wife I can draw a direct line to violating one or more of these qualities. However, every successful relationship I have ever come across had these qualities within the individuals as well as the marriage itself.

The plan is that we would seek to know and embody the character qualities needed to make relationships all that God intended them to be. Specifically:

*"Finally brethren, whatever is **true**, whatever is **honorable**, whatever is **right**, whatever is **pure**, whatever is **lovely**, whatever is of **good report**, if there is any excellence and if anything worthy of praise, dwell on these things."* (Phil. 4:8)

These verses go on to state that we should dwell on these qualities and practice them continually. Let's take a brief look at each to get a general idea of what it looks like. (I took one each day and spent some time dwelling on how I could better embody each quality.

Whatever is true / honest. Ask the tough questions. Do I have a tendency to tell half truths to cover ourselves? Do I exaggerate? Do I sometimes talk around issues to hide areas of our lives? God made it clear to me as I thought about being truthful in every area of my life, even recreation.

I love to play golf, but one of the toughest things to do in golf is to be honest about your score. Grown men all of a sudden have trouble counting. It is embarrassing to be the only person to be honest enough to say, yeah, I had a 13 on that hole when everyone else has rationalized their way down to a 5 or 6. We live in a society that has moved from being honest at all cost to one that encourages to be honest until it costs us, and then rationalize. When we commit ourselves to becoming the truth we have committed to the plan of becoming what God desires.

Whatever is honorable. This is a good opportunity to not only examine ourselves, but also our spouses. Those who are honorable have a good track record with friends, in loyalty, trust, and confidentiality. A great question to ask with regard to someone being honorable is, "What was it about your spouse that really made you think he/she was above the rest?" That is the quality you honored. Honor is such a critical quality. I have seen it over and over in relationships at all levels. When feelings fail, character continues. Consider how you can appreciate that quality in him or her again. How can you draw it out and encourage it?

What is right. General Norman Swartzkoff summed it up when he said, "I don't have trouble knowing what is right, my trouble comes in doing what I already know is right." Not once in my walk with the Lord have I come across a situation or a decision that I was not able to find out what was right.

What is right does not come from some super spiritual procedure. When we invite Christ into our lives He is there. When we ask Him to show us what is right with a sensitive, obedient attitude, He will. Another clue to knowing what is right is if we find ourselves wasting time trying to define what is right, instead of doing what we know has always been right, we are almost always going to be wrong. People who we can count on to do what is right in any circumstances are such a blessing. They know what God's plan is all about Are you such a person?

Whatever is pure. Chapter 7 will give more practical insight on purity, but let's take a quick look at two aspects. One, the Bible gives very clear directions on purity (II Tim. 2:22, Ex. 20:14, Heb. 13:4). The plan is to follow God's definition and become it. Your past may or may not be marked with impurity, but God has already dealt with your past and forgiven it. If we are to experience relationships to the fullness of His plan, we must properly deal with then forget what lies behind and reach forward to what lies ahead (Phil.3:13-14).

The commitment we have to make is for now and from now on to be pure.

Whatever is lovely. This quality at first glance seems the most elusive. My friends gave me great insight on this one. Lovely is the dream. Compare yourself, your interest, and your relationships to your dream situation. Don't settle for less than God's best. My friend Stan encouraged me to marry over my head. He reminded me that we marry for life so aim high. My wife is far beyond my dreams and is the definition of lovely. I second the advice about lovely: Compare to the dream, don't settle, and never stop working the dream marriage.

The final quality of the plan is *good report*. This is an easy one to start thinking about. Let's look at a couple angles. Find a few close committed friends and go over these character qualities. Ask them to rate you from 1 to 10 on each. Another angle to consider is often the areas we are most critical of in others reveal the areas most needing work in our lives. Finally, what is your own report? Is it good? When talking to others do you find yourself giving good reports of your spouse and marriage, or apologizing for parts or the whole?

Please realize God's plan is much deeper and more personally intricate then we will ever be able to discover. His plan is 100% perfect for our situations. The way we implement the plan is simple to understand. At the end of verse 8, Paul tells us to dwell on these things. That is exactly the first step in the plan. Take your life and situation. Pray for God to reveal the areas you need work on and how to build the qualities we just discussed. Consider each quality and I am sure you will add dozens of ideas and insights to every one of mine.

After the ideas begin to flow, it is time for the second step in implementing God's plan. Verse 9 includes the key phrase, "Practice these things." Some areas will go smoothly, others with difficulty. The promise God makes us is that He will personally be there to walk with us through it all. What a blessing! The God who shows us the way will guide us through it.

When we decide we want to pursue relationships the right way, all we have to do to begin is pick up the plan. No more waiting around hoping to one day find that nebulous love. We can start following the plan today. Building the character needed. Become the love we are looking for.

RECONNECTING

Discussion / Action

1. Describe a time when you tried out for, or applied for something you really wanted and you got it.

2. Read Philippians 4:8 (page 56). Share with your spouse which of these 2 qualities best describe him or her.

3. Together decide which two qualities best describe your marriage.

4. When comparing your marriage to the list is there any area that needs more work than the others do?

5. What is one way to improve that area this week?

¹NAS

CHAPTER SEVEN

Where Am I?

Exact Directions to Complete Love

*W*omen (on average) are not good at giving directions...except to other women. The conversation usually goes something like, "Okay, you go... um, oh, I know, you go down that road..." You know THAT road? Another woman will stand there and due to the inflection or body language or some communication lacking in men will say, "Yeah! THAT road!" Then they will go on describing trees and houses and say things like, when you FEEL like you have gone too far, turn left. If women were the only ones allowed to drive we could save billions on road signs. Many women don't give great directions, but because most men don't take directions it works out fine.

Fortunately for men and women God's directions are simple, easy to understand and when we follow them, they get us to where we want to go. The reason many people never experience lasting love is because they don't follow directions. God's directions pick up in II Peter 1:5-9.

Where we are to dwell on and practice God's plan, we are also to seek His directions by "applying all diligence." So much for sitting back and complaining about our spouses short comings. The ball is in our court to get up and follow the directions. II Peter 1:5-7 gives us the directions to Love.

"Now for this very reason also, applying all diligence,
in your faith supply moral excellence, and
in your moral excellence, knowledge, and
in your knowledge, self-control, and
in your self-control, perseverance, and
in your perseverance, godliness, and
in your godliness, brotherly kindness, and
in your brotherly kindness, LOVE."

Where does the road to real love start? With moral excellence. Would you describe your life as morally excellent? If so great! (I realized I needed work on this area of my life or I would never experience the joy of Godly love.) God in His grace simply allowed me to see where I needed to start.

Any time we ask for directions the first question is usually, where are you coming from? We cannot give directions without knowing the point of origin. Some of you reading this will review these qualities and be well on your way. I encourage you at this point to not skip any of the direction. Take your time and pray through each of them. Skipping any area listed here would be as ludicrous as missing a turn and thinking, "I'll just take the next part of the directions and we will be fine." NO, you will be lost.

The flow of these qualities is there for a reason. Again, you will find much more than I ever could, but here are some starting insights. Follow along in your Bible if you would like (II Peter 1:5-7) Diligence is a must. Just reading this one time and agreeing with it won't change anything. Starting point: *Moral excellence.* Do I embody the qualities mentioned in Phil. 4:8-9? Would I describe my current view of my actions and thoughts pure? Many people think they can compromise this one area and God's grace and forgiveness will just take care of it.

Knowledge. Open up God's word and diligently find the answers. We will always move toward what we focus on. If we focus solely on our feelings and hormonal reaction, guess what? We won't become morally excellent. If we allow our focus to be constantly drawn away by the media or a number of other distractions we can easily get derailed. In II Peter 1:9 it gives the results for all who choose not to take God's directions. Those who lack these qualities become blind or short-sighted. There are numbers of blind and short sighted people in marriages today. We have to begin to see there is a direct correlation to what we choose to focus on and the results. This was never more apparent to me than after returning one weekend from a trip. Every person I know considers himself or herself basically moral. I have even talked to people in the middle of cheating on a spouse who would never describe him or herself as immoral. I also have to confess that I too can rationalize a lot of thoughts and behaviors by proclaiming no lines were crossed or people hurt. The question we have to face is the second word here, "excellence." Are my thoughts, feelings, actions, and every part of me morally excellent? If we are honest there is room to grow before we can say we are completely there. How exactly can we get to this level of excellence? We need to know more of what it means to be excellent.

I visited my wife's parents several times before we got married. They have a very nice guest bedroom with it's own bathroom. Men occasionally read in bathrooms. I don't know where the custom started, but I feel obligated to keep up the tradition. The problem is that my in-laws only had decorating magazines in the bathroom.

I began reading the decorating magazines. (You have to read something in there.) I had no idea that those times in their restroom was having a effect on me until one Monday night. There we were in my friend's living room about to watch a football game. It was a guy's night in a guy's house. During conversation before kickoff, my mind wandered and I had an idea that I almost shared with the guys.

They stopped and said, "Did you want to say something?" I nodded that I didn't.

What I had almost blurted out in the middle of guy's night was, "Wow, this room would look really good with some window treatments and a nice chair rail border." Can you believe that? It was then that I realized what we focus on we move toward. Knowledge alone is not enough.

The writer of II Peter drives us on to realize knowledge without action does not work. There are many days I get home from work or a trip and the last thing I want to do is WORK on my marriage. I don't have the energy to do anything much less think about the wonderful principle from a lesson or book and go encourage my wife with my newfound expertise. Then I realize what I am feeling is a total lack of self-control. More often than not I am not physically spent or mentally gone. If I had the opportunity to get in nine holes before lights out I could make it happen. It is just that I have poured into a day and "I" want to vegetate in front of something that requires no feedback what so ever. *Self-control* is taking those moments and choosing to control them instead of them controlling me. I am not for two seconds going to tell you it is easy. Nor am I going to tell you endless success stories. I will say those times are what make the difference in a good marriage verses a bad marriage, a good relationship with your wife and a anywhere, anytime, anything you want big boy, connection with your wife. I am not there yet.

When we find the knowledge and start to apply it we will quickly discover that action goes against our nature. It takes great self-control. Even when we diligently apply self-control, there may be some bumps in the road. That is when perseverance kicks in. *Perseverance* is the point where we don't feel like doing the right thing any more but keep doing it anyway. This is the point where there is no turning back. We trust God despite the circumstance.

When we reach this point we begin to see *godliness*. We begin to understand. The next stage is to combat staying in this stage and proceed to – brotherly kindness. God knows what a false sense of pride can do. There are many people not experiencing love in relationships because they have chosen to stop at this point and glory in their godliness. It is much easier to look down on a spouse than to move forward by getting on his or her level.

I have to speak in the masculine here due to my experience. I know men more interested in appearing righteous and godly to those around them then showing simple kindness to a spouse who is struggling at home. These men serve on committees, lead bible studies, and hold positions of success. None of which are bad in and of themselves. But, when those take priority over being willing and ready to roll up sleeves to clean up diapers, vacuum floors or any other household chore they form a pious and empty godliness. Brotherly kindness is a conscience effort to go below the surface in a relationship and connect by communicating with our words, attitude and actions, "How can I help make your world better?" "You are more important than anything else in the world to me." We used to think that while dating. If we choose to prove it now when we may or may not feel like it then we are going to find out what genuine love is all about. Relate to the trials and pain. There is no quality more like Jesus himself than *brotherly kindness*. There is also something magical and attractive about anyone who is willing to give while expecting nothing in return. Some of the greatest connecting times for a couple will be while serving others together. Love is the natural by-product by serving.

If these directions seem a bit lofty, they are. When we seek with all diligence, trusting in Christ we will be able to effectively reach this type of love, pushing past what we are capable of on our own. Bart Starr, the former quarterback and coach of the Green Bay Packers, puts it in perspective, "Strive for perfection. Not that perfection is obtainable, but by striving for perfection we achieve excellence." God goes one better. He promises to walk with us and perfect us until Christ returns. This process showed me clearly that what we think, we do. Our actions determine our habits. Our habits define our character, and our character determines our destiny.

I love the way II Peter 1:8-9 describes the results of our choosing the perfecting process. In verse 8 it says, "If these qualities are yours and are increasing, they render you neither useless nor unfruitful."[1] So we will not be useless and unfruitful. That does not seem like much of a reward for all that work. It took a while before I got the hang of this seemingly insignificant result. What I found was that when these qualities exist and increase, the natural result is being useful and fruitful. It is effortless. It is as if God is telling us to focus on the directions and He will take care of all the rest.

God's Plan and Directions can and will lead us to the type of marriage we desire.

We must discipline ourselves to embody these qualities, because it is discipline and not desire that determines destiny.

RECONNECTING

1. What is the most lost you have ever been?

2. Look at II Peter I: 5-7 (page 61). Where is your marriage on this continuum?

   Morally Excellent: We are committed to one another and the marriage.

   Knowledge: We are learning how to make our marriage better.

   Self-control: We make the effort regularly to improve the quality of our relationship.

   Perseverance: We do not always click but we actively keep trying to improve.

   Godliness: We sacrificially give to one another even when feelings are not there.

   Brotherly Kindness: All the above happen but mainly we just love being around one another.

   Love: The commitment during all these phases. Until we pass through each, love is not really complete.

3. What do you see as the greatest benefit to the stage you are in right now?

4. Tell your spouse one reason why you are glad to be going through this stage together.

5. Recall a time when you went through a difficult time together. What did you appreciate most about having your spouse there?

SECTION THREE

RECONNECTING OUR
Actions

*W*hat kind of marriage do you want? How about a marriage of love, joy, and peace? A spouse who is patient, kind, and gentle. What about a relationship marked by faithfulness, godliness, and self-control? It sounds pretty good doesn't it? If you offered this to people, most would accept. The answer is the same as the answer to my sixteenth birthday. (It is a stretch, but hang with me.)

A sixteen year old male wants to drive. A few days before my 16th birthday my father asked me if I would like a car when I turned sixteen. His question was met with an obvious, "Yeah!" Much to my shock He asked the exciting question, "What kind would you like?"

My mind began to race. I would spare him the Ferrari and go for the more practical 300ZX. After sharing my dream he asked what color, and why the 300ZX? The explanation was well received and everything was going great until my bubble burst. My father responded, "That sounds great! How are you going to be able to afford such a nice car?"

My dream ended more abruptly than it had begun. I told him I couldn't afford it. My father then explained a lesson of life I am still learning. "You can afford one, but it will cost you. You will have to work hard and save every penny. In a few years you could buy the car." I had to decide if a new car was worth the effort, time, and sacrifice.

A relationship marked by love, joy, peace, patience, kindness, goodness, faithfulness, and self- control is far more valuable than any car will ever be. The tragic lesson to learn is that many people do not want to put in the time and effort to make it happen. This section is about the plan and the promise to those who choose to desire God's best. Galatians 6:7 puts it all into perspective. *"Do not be deceived: God cannot be mocked. A man reaps what he sows."* What are you sowing? Are you sowing?

The stages listed below show a practical application of the truths we have already discussed. If you have ever wanted clarity or direction on how to nourish a healthy relationship, these stages will help. There is no magic here, rather a guide to turn us to God, trust in His truth, ask for His wisdom and see His will unfold before you. Once the desire is determined, these directions will add the clarity needed to make progress in the relationship maze.

CHAPTER EIGHT

Becoming A Great Lover

*Equations To Becoming
A Great Lover*

*G*od wants you to be a great lover. The Bible (yes, the Bible) makes it known to us, and we are going to take a very close look into fulfilling this glorious task. The difficulty in these equations is not in the understanding of the qualities involved, but in the discipline in carrying them out. Use a cheat sheet if you would like, but do not misunderstand the clear qualities involved in becoming a great lover.

I know several men after hearing this title will tell their friends or spouse, "He wrote this chapter about ME." I sincerely hope that is true. Lets go ahead and work through the chapter anyway so in case I missed something you can let me know.

My father did a great job letting me know about the important issues in life. When I was 13 my father was bold enough to have "The TALK" with me. He shared how women and men are different. There is a very strong drive in men that can control us. It is something that while women experience a similar feeling men are far more driven by it. He said, "Son, I think you know what I am talking about. Men need... the remote control!" He continued, "We have a sixth sense that needs to be developed. It is the ability to sit in a room full of people and with out ever looking around be able to sense when someone is actually getting interested in the program and...change the channel!" I have struggled in my marriage to relinquish control to my wife on occasion. She simply has not got that innate ability to surf during commercials and return to a game before the next drive, inning, or quarter starts. It really is about control.

My father also had a wonderful talk about control in the area of sex. He shared the basics and asked open ended questions that led me to understand the reasons why marriage was the place to experience the joy of sex without the disease, fear, and regret that so many have had to endure. As a 13-year-old I did not really have a lot of opportunity to compromise the wisdom he shared but his words would come to mind on many occasions in the future.

I practiced more self-control then I ever thought possible. There were serious relationships that progressed to the point where I wanted to cross certain lines I when knew in my heart it would not be the right time. Practicing self-control then was seldom easy.

After marriage and the enjoyment of the sexual aspect of marriage I am sincerely thankful for the control God enabled me to display. I was certainly not perfect nor did I always understand the why to wait idea, but in every instance I chose to do it God's way I look back with great thankfulness. So why do I share this at a time when 99% of you reading this are married and there is nothing we can do about our past accept maybe deal with feelings of regret, resting in God's forgiveness and moving forward.

The reason I bring it up is for us to remember the difficulty of self-control in this area. I am sure there are couple who never struggled with waiting until marriage to have sex and that it was never an issue. I am so happy for those 3 couples. I guess arranged marriages are good for a few things. For the rest of us that internal longing and intel-lectual reconciliation were very real. No matter what your choice was then God has a plan now. The plan is for us to show self-control in an entirely new realm. Instead of a restrained self-control we are now called to a proactive control of our bodies and relationship.

Proactive control of sex? Sign me up!

Actually it is a proactive self-control over how we love our spouse that as a wonderful side effect can and will take the sexual aspect of a mar-riage to a better level for both partners. It is the process of becoming a great lover. Take these truths to heart and your spouse will be brag-ging about you everywhere. Practice these principles and instead of you thinking of yourself as the greatest your spouse will think you are the greatest lover ever.

What are these quailites and how does this work? The answer is found in I Corinthians 13:4-8a.

When most Christians hear that scripture reference they think 'The Love Chapter.' You are correct. When God first laid this equation on my heart I thought the same thing and began to intellectually tune out. Then the Lord rocked me with an uncomfortable set of thoughts. Before I could open to the passage I had to answer some very painful questions.

Genuine Love is something we strongly desire, but too often we do not even know how to define. I am embarrassed to think I desired love in my life, but did not even know completely what love was. It can be painfully evident that too often we know where to find a certain truth, we know about it, and have even taken part of it to heart, but fail to regularly live it out.

We will take a brief look at the qualities defining God's definition of Love, but before we do, can you name all of them? I am embarrassed to say that I have read that passage hundreds of times, had it quoted at my wedding, know exactly where it is, agree with every bit of it but could not tell you how many qualities were mentioned. Can you guess how many there are? Without looking, list as many qualities of love as you think are in the passage we are about to learn.

Now look up I Corinthians 13:4-7 in your Bible or simply continue to read. How did you do?

This passage provides such a versatile definition. It was written to the church at Corinth with regard to the love God desires all believers to have within any church body. These components of love can be applied in a huge variety of marital situations. See if you can find a need for application in one of these I WISH situations.

I WISH I had a loving marriage that met the desire I have within me.

I WISH my marriage was more like it was at first.

I WISH my spouse understood and loved me more.

This passage and these qualities fulfill every one of those wishes, but in a very different way than one might think.

The natural view of love is to enjoy what we get out of it. God's qualities are first and foremost what we give, not get, out of love. The answer to fulfilling our wish is not determined by the uncontrollable whims of someone else. The magic of this wish lies within us. Do we have the desire and discipline to know and practice these qualities of love and thus become the very person God desires us to be? Is it not interesting that so many of us want a growing, lasting, fulfilling love, but do not even know what it is? The world's greatest lover will not only know, but will embody these factors as well. Let's take a brief look at them.

Patience or long suffering. This is an infinite capacity to endure.

Kindness or mercy. Now the patience thing is okay, but this word 'kindness' is just a bit too difficult to swallow. Kind does not simply mean to be nice whenever possible. This word in its original context means something far more. Picture if you will someone giving you a gift you really wanted. Now picture how you would feel knowing you had already bought the gift they wanted and needed most in the whole world and joyfully lavished it upon them in reciprocation. The kindness mentioned here is that joyous response but to the opposite prompt.

What the apostile Paul is saying in this verse is when someone treats you badly, you treat them with a joyous, need -meeting response. I don't know about you, but that is just not natural. Oh, sure I can be mistreated by other people and not complain, but push the wrong buttons too many times and you would have wished you hadn't. This qualities is challenging us to resist reaction and respond to ill treatment with joyous care.

Then Paul goes into a list of selfish factors that really hit the very nature of most of our actions. *Love is not jealous.* There is no competition in love. So much for the "all is fair in love and war" philosophy. Love looks out for someone's good without regard for self. Even the conversation focuses on others. *Love does not brag and is not arrogant.* True love is more interested in giving praise and attention than gaining anything. Then there is the action factor. *Love is not unbecoming* and *does not seek its own favor.* Love seeks first, foremost, and always the good of others in approach and actions. By putting others in the spotlight, love acts honorably to shed light on those around. Love's purpose is always the edification and illumination of others.

Paul not only shares how to give the proper actions, he also illustrates how not to take the improper actions. *Love is not provoked* and *does not take into account a wrong suffered.* Instantly several circumstances come to mind where I have been wronged. This quality of love accounts only the good and relinquishes all debts. Along with the forgiving all debts comes the mind set of never allowing new debts to occur. Love is never touchy and doesn't allow anything to lessen its focus on giving wholeheartedly.

Love's wholehearted quality is also not influenced by outside sources. *Love does not rejoice in unrighteousness, but rejoices in the truth.*

Our society has become overwhelmed by violence and suffering. The newsrooms of today live for any immoral or evil headline. Christ lived in a time of turmoil yet walked, lived, and breathed peace. Rejoicing in the truth is to ask the questions, "What would Jesus do, say, think?"

Then there are my favorite factors of all. *Bears all things, Believes all things, Hopes all things, Endures all things.* The word 'bears' denotes a conscience choice to cover. Love is not blind; it knows what is really there, but chooses to cover it up permanently. Love doesn't stop with simply forgiving the past. Believes all things says, "Your slate is clean with me and you are free."

Junior high was not a time of liberty for me. It seems teachers from year to year pass on the names of who they think are the problem students. My name topped that list in seventh grade. The first week of school I was put in the hot seat in every class except one. Mrs. Cherry's science class was my haven and my chance to start all over. She lived out the quality of believing the good in everyone. I remember the first day of her class. She announced, "All of you have a clean slate with me. As far as I am concerned you are all wonderful until you prove me otherwise."

I would have died before proving her wrong. She gave me a chance to live up to her expectations, not my past. After a few months, I got kind of comfortable in my new found graces. A homework assignment was too long and bothersome, so my best friend and I decided to do opposite halfs and copy the other's work. We thought we were so smart until we were asked to stay behind after class the day after we turned in the homework.

Mrs. Cherry lived the true meaning of love once again. She didn't cut us any slack, rather she called us on it and gave us both zeros. My greatest fear was being realized. I had failed again and had proven her wrong. I was a no good cheat, and she had proof.

Then love hoped all things. Not in a gullible optimistic way, but in a tough and tender balance. She said the words that broke my heart and healed it all at once, "I am so disappointed in you. I never thought you of all people would do something like this." My heart was broken. She went on, "I know this is not you. I will give you a zero this time, but you are never going to do this again. You know better and this just is not the way you are." My heart healed with a second chance. Leon Morris puts it beautifully, "Hoping all things means to never take failure as final."[2]

The final quality is the effort of love. Endures all things does not mean a resigned patience, but an active, consistent, steady plodding forward. The picture painted here is one of a military leader going into battle. Amidst the worst of circumstances, he remains completely focused on advancing. With explosions all around and fear about to burst within, he presses forward. Love certainly endures. It is with this quality we have a choice to make. Will we endure? The truth is clear. The equation is set. The qualities are faultless. We are committed to know, do, and become love.

The steps in this equation are very simple, but hard to embody. First, understand this is a definition of how completely God loves us. He chooses to cover our faults; He believes not what we are, but what He has made us to become. He refuses to take failure as final, and He endures to the bitter end regardless of the circumstances. His is the love that does not fail. God longs for you and I to become that same love. Choosing to understand His love is the first step, comprehension.

The second step is application. James 1:22-25 challenges us perfectly. Are we going to be an effectual doer or a forgetful hearer? Will we be the type that accepts and believes the truth and with a complete understanding places these qualities into our lives? Do you really want to be a great lover? The benefits are out of this world. Just attempting to transform will bring wonderful results.

One of the most practical applications I have seen is to take one quality per day and simply do it. There is a group of teachers who heard this point and took it to heart. They shared with me their method of taking one quality per day and holding each other accountable to applying it. This process goes on for thirty days (each quality twice). What a great way to put it into practice! The equation is simple: Truth + Application + Honest Evaluation + Reconciliation back to the Truth = Love that Never Fails.

If we genuinely desire a marriage that will never fail, we must learn these qualities and become these qualities. God desires us to be the world's greatest lovers. The challenge is set, and the truth is clear. Will you do it?

RECONNECTING

Discussion / Action

1. Name a time other than your wedding day when you felt how great your love can be.

2. Give two reasons why you love your spouse.

3. Read I Corinthians 13:4-7. Which three qualities best describe your spouse?

4. Share which quality you feel is your weakest. What is one way to improve that area?

---

[1] The book of Ruth.

[2] Morris, Leon. *Tyndale New Testament Commentaries*;
(Grand Rapids, MI: W.M.B. EERDMANS PUB. Co. 1961) p.186.

CHAPTER NINE

Completely Trusting

Pursuit Principles

*I*t happens every four years to anyone in the state of Georgia who wants to operate some kind of motor vehicle. It was time to renew my license and I had the perfect plan. I'd drop off Heather's car at the repair shop (someone decided to run a red light and reconstruct the front side of her car), have a friend take me to the car rental place, and finally cruise by the new "express renewal" post and be completely done by lunch to properly enjoy my birthday.

The first step came off without a hitch. On to the car rental. That's when the fun began. After filling out countless forms and promising them my first born male child, I was ready for my next chore until... "Excuse me Mr. Kington, but did you know your license expires today?" said the surprised clerk holding the keys to my freedom.

I confirmed his observation and shared with him my plan to have my license renewed and explained how the license was good at least until midnight. "This rental is for 24 hours and your license will be void for part of your rental if for any reason you cannot renew. I cannot rent you this car."

To make a long story somewhat shorter, my friend ran me over to the **express** renewal location which of course had major computer problems. After forty-five minutes the **express** renewal post had not even processed one person in the line of over twenty. I was number eighteen. We proceeded to the main license office some twenty-five minutes away only to realize it was closed on Mondays. Of course my birthday was on a Monday.

We traveled back to the **express** renewal location to find the line had not moved in the past hour and was now longer, and I was late for my lunch appointment. One futile attempt after another and I gave up on getting a new license for Monday.

The next day I got up early dropped my wife off at work and set out to become a legal driver once again. Another marathon line and close encounter with the wonders of technology and speed of a bureaucracy that supposedly makes life easier. I finally had my new license!

There were several times I considered just being a renegade and going without a valid operating license. My conscience and luck combined would not allow it, so I persevered and now I have the official certificate to drive.

I actually pondered during the ordeal why it was happening.

I remember praying, "Lord why can't everything go smoothly and allow me to enjoy my birthday?" (As if being born has special privileges and rights that should accompany it.) The question that continued to come to mind was, "Is it worth it? Was all the hassle worth the privilege of driving?"

I evaluated the options and quickly decided it beat the alternatives by a long shot. Sure I would much rather drive than walk, ride my bike, run, take the bus, or any combination of the above. Yes it is actually worth the runaround, the lines, the aggravation.

Many people philosophically agree with the ideas of what God's truth says about relationships. Many will even read this book and intellectually agree with most if not all of its premise. The frustration comes when we have to live it out in our day to day lives. Proverbs 3:5-7 says, *"Trust in the Lord with all your heart and lean not on your own understanding. In all your ways acknowledge Him, and He will make your path straight."* We must come to the point where we decide yes, it is worth trusting His way over what I think, feel, or reason.

In marriage, this place of completely trusting is initially easy. Then time passes and life can turn in a myriad of directions. The question will come to mind. Does God really know what He is doing? Is trusting this person really worth it? Does God really want me to endure this? I do not pretend to know your circumstances. I do however know God does know them and He is very clear on what is worth trusting. His word about your situation is a wonderful place to start. We must start asking the question, do I completely trust God in my marriage? I must learn to completely trust Him.

While running one day I saw a wonderful picture of what complete trust looks like. The river I run along has a few bridges that span creeks. While running up to one such bridge and then over it, I came across a father and his one-year old son. The son was standing on the handrail while the father held tightly to his shirt and trousers. The father would allow his son to lean forward and hang in the balance over the water while the son shrieked with joy and laughter. The father pulled his son back and enjoyed the moment with him. They repeated this while I jogged by.

Though the bridge was only about seven feet high, I began to figure out how high that would be compared to you and me, roughly fifty feet. Now imagine standing on a ledge fifty feet up; a friend grabs you tightly by the belt and says, "Go ahead, lean out, I've got you!" I have some strong friends that love me very much, but I would have to say no! I don't think so. There are so many variables, I just don't trust my life to someone in that situation. It's not worth it. But to a little boy who trusted that his father was in complete control, it was the time of his life! Joy beyond measure!

Our God is infinitely trustworthy, and when He says to trust in Him with ALL your heart and in ALL your way acknowledge Him, we can take Him at His word. I am afraid my way is quite different. Mine is too often to look at what I understand and what I think and what I want and ask God to give me ALL His resources to do what I determine needs to be done. I hope you see as you read this how ludicrous that sounds.

One of the first determinations we have to make is that we don't know everything, but He does. I must come to Him for the answers and trust that His way is, will be, and always has been better than anything I could come up with.

This concept was never more obvious then when a friend and I decided to start a workout program. We met at the gym and he asked, "What do you think we should do?" I am a man so I have an answer to any question (I did not say I have the right answer just an answer). I answered with my thoughts and insights on a balanced workout and in about two minutes exhausted my knowledge of the topic. The plan was set. We worked out anyway.

The drive home after our exercise was a bit humbling. As I reflected on the workout I realized some painful realities. First, he had beaten me at every competitive exercise. I don't like to lose and God chose to use this to get my attention. Then God began to prompt my thoughts to help me realize how selfish and deeply rooted my lack of complete trust.

Looking at Tom, (the friend I had worked out with) he is taller, stronger, and in far better shape. Tom played college football as a quarterback and has maintained the physique to prove it. He rides his bike regularly and basically puts me to shame as an athlete. I am in shape; it is just that my shape is more the shape of a pear. I make it one trip up and down the basketball court and I am looking for oxygen. I realized while driving home as God whispered in my heart, "Kenn who needs to be deciding what workout to do, you or Tom?"

If I desire to get into better shape I might want to start listening and stop talking. If I genuinely desire to be in a growing , loving, fulfilling marriage, I need to quit telling God what to do and start trusting His truth that has been proven over the course of time. God created marriage. Maybe, just maybe He knows a little more about how to make it the best it can be. We must make the transition from trusting our own thoughts, feeling, and abilities, to completely trust the all-knowing trustworthy God of all.

To completely trust does not mean merely seeing what to trust; trust is an action. We do not completely trust anything until we act upon that trust. Too many people sit on the sidelines knowing what is right, hearing God's truth every week, and agreeing that what He says is true, but never making the transition from their minds into their lives.

The reason most church members today look like they just sucked on a bad lemon instead of appearing to have been filled with the abundant life provided them through Christ, because they do not act on the truth they already know. The problem with most marriages is not that we don't know enough, but we get lazy in not doing enough of what we already know to be right. We cannot say we completely trust God's truth until we start acting upon it.

God's truth is not unlike the greatest amusement park ride. We cannot and will not enjoy a roller coaster until we get on it. We can sit outside, watch, and say, "Wow, that looks like fun." We may even get closer and stand at the end of the ride watching people come off and hearing them recount the different turns and hills. Listening closely, we hear the distant screams and laughter as the train roars up, down, and around the tracks.

As observers we can even agree with one another and proclaim, "Roller coasters are fun!!" However, we simply can't enjoy the thrill of a roller coaster unless we get in line and actually get on the ride. Only then will we experience the anticipation of the first hill, the rush of emotion wondering if this thing really is on the tracks, the fright of being completely out of control, and yet loving every minute of it. There is no real joy until you and I get on the ride.

The ride to finding real love in a marriage is no different. We may study about marriage until our eyes cross, but until we are willing to completely trust that truth and start putting it into practice, it is worthless. Completely trusting means just that, completely. Too often I have started the process and after a few failures or difficult circumstances, it's back to learning more and just forgetting about the application. We just hope some of the truth rubs off on us and by osmosis becomes part of us and renders the results we desire. It's just not going to happen! Is it easy? No. Will we falter? Yes. Is it natural? No. Is it worth it? YES!

I remember the first year of our marital bliss and the people I call "Killjoys" that occasionally crossed our path. "You must be newly-weds! Just wait a few years you'll get over it." Get over it so we can do what? Be bitter, crotchety, and miserable. No thanks. I think I will continue to try and stay in the honey moon phase if it is all the same to you. It is not easy to continue getting on the ride of trust and truth. It takes effort. But those sad examples of misery keep me getting back to the truth and trying a little harder.

There is another extreme from that same group of people who have been married for a while. My wife and I were involved in a newlywed's class for a few years. The class was led by a couple that was 20 years our senior. They were in a wonderfully mature phase of being on a honeymoon. They were very open and honest about the struggles, challenges, and realities of marriage but had a funda-mental joy about their relationship. I asked one time why they were so giving to our class. They share how they were there for selfish reasons. "You guys keep us young and focused on what marriage is suppose to be." They continued, "The older couples here (at our church) just complain and moan. You guys have fun and really know how to show love to each other." Ken and Sherry really had it figured out. Ken even shared in our men's group one time how he got ideas from listening to us and used them with Sherry. I want to be like that after 25 years of marriage.

How can we maintain focus like the second couple and remain on a honeymoon for 25+ years? By taking what we have already gone over in the previous chapters and keep putting it into our lives. Daily we must take a portion and ask God how we can live it today. Look at I Corinthians 13: 4-7 and ask God to show you which of the fifteen qualities of love to embody today. Look at Philippians 4:8 and ask God which qualities you need to be dwelling on today. Look at II Peter 1:5-8 and ask God to show you which actions need to increase in your life today. We must come to the point where practicing God's truth becomes second nature. It is when we practice His truth that we will establish our complete trust in Him and begin to experience the fulfillment, joy, peace, and other attributes God always intended us to experience.

My wife and I recently experienced roller coasters for the first time in several years. As we entered the park, I was excited and could only remember the thrills. As a ten year old, my friend and I would go to the park early and ride until the fireworks were over and the park closed. That thrill was replaced with reality on the first hill of the first ride. I began to question the construction of the structure. The safety of the ride was heavy on my mind. The height we had climbed to was way more than I remembered. Instead of raising both hands in a symbol of freedom, I gripped the lap bar with white knuckles. Why? Why was I sitting in total discomfort while two teenagers in front of me laughed with their hands in the air with reckless abandon as I once did? They were accustomed to the ride. God is wooing us to trust Him with that same abandon and experience the same joy. Wait in the line (know His truth). Get on the ride (Put His truth into action). Ride it for all it is worth (See that He is completely trust worthy).

RECONNECTING

Discussion / Action

1. Name your favorite amusement park ride and tell why.

2. Identify something your spouse does regularly that you like.

3. Name something you enjoyed that your spouse did more when you were dating than he or she does now.

4. As a couple is there any area you could or should be more trusting or God? Talk about how to take one step toward trust Him more.

CHAPTER TEN

How About Those Fries?

Diligently Waiting

*H*ave you ever received bad service at a restaurant? I mean really bad. One restaurant topped them all for me. It got to the point of actually being funny. The setting is simple enough. Heather and I were grabbing a bite between speaking engagements. We were not in a rush but neither was our waitress.

After wondering if we had mistakenly sat in the Bermuda Triangle, our waitress decided to break away from her friends and stop by our table. We had decided to go ahead and order more than just our drinks for the fear that we might not see our little helper again. It was a good decision too. She decided to vanish again after dropping off our drinks, and we began to wonder if we had been forgotten.

About thirty minutes later she surfaced again and asked if we needed anything. Dinner, would be nice. "Oh", she said, "I'll be right back with that." Our glasses also had been long since drained of any liquid when what was supposed to be our dinner arrived. Our favorite item from this particular restaurant was their fries. We'd ordered double fries and had gotten none. She dropped the plates on the table and headed away asking rhetorically, "Is there anything else you need?"

"My fries would be nice, and if we could get a refill on drinks that would be great." With a wink and a turn she was gone again. A several minutes later she looked at our table while passing by.

"You guys need anything?"

" Yeah, some refills would be nice and my fries?"

"Oh, sure," with a smile she said, "I'll have that right out for you."

Once again she asked as she passed by, "Anything else?"

"Could I get you to check on my fries?"

"Sure thing!" She smiled, winked and walked away.

Don't get me wrong, I was happy to have the ice to chew on and the burger, but after waiting well over an hour it didn't seem too much to ask for what I had ordered.

To top it off, I watched her walk away from our table and go straight to where her friends were standing. There they stood not even close to the kitchen and my long forgotten fries. She never even checked.

After investing a small portion of our lives, we had to go. I motioned for her and she made time in her busy schedule to stop by our table. "Was everything alright? Can I get you two anything else?" she said with a sincere smile and a wink.

"No, we sort of need to get going, so if we could get the check that would be all. Oh, we never got our fries so if you could knock those off the bill that would be good."

"Oh, do you want them to go?" she actually said with concern.

"No, I really don't have the time now. She was back in about five more minutes and we were off. The fries that never showed up. The sincere waitress who never put one and one together.

Heather and I laughed about that for days. Her continual, "Can I get you anything?" and smile, wink, walk away was unbelievable.

It was a few days after that when I ran across James 1:22. I wanted to have it mounted and give it to our waitress friend. "But prove yourselves doers of the word and not merely hearers who delude themselves." It was at that time the phrase "wait upon the Lord" took on an entirely new meaning. I realized with great pain that this waitress had illustrated how I often approached the Lord; how I "wait on Him."

With a pure heart I say, Lord teach me your truth. Show me Your way. How can I be a better Husband? What in my life needs to change? Then in the most sincere way possible, I agree in my heart with His truth, smile, wink, and turn to go on my way completely forgetting what just happened. For too long I suffered from a condition that so many struggle with. We want to serve God. We desire to experience marriage and all parts of life the way He intended, but we fail to put one and one together. The results in transforming our relationships will not come from increasing the amount of knowledge we have about them. Results will come when we begin to diligently wait upon the Lord.

We must learn to shift our view of waiting from an outward observation of which we have no control to an inward evaluation for change. If you can picture in your mind coming to the Lord each day as a waiter or waitress, "Lord, what would you like me to change in my life today? What area of my character needs work? How can I more clearly communicate to my spouse how much I love her? Father, what verse do I need to embody more today?" Then take His truth as an effectual doer and not a forgetful hearer. In every passage we have gone over in this book the principle of diligently waiting (or effectively doing) is the foundation.

In II Peter 1:5 the key to the process of love is given, *"Now for this very reason also, applying all diligence..."*[1] I Corinthians 13:7 describes one of the most important aspects of love as, *"endures all things."* In Philippians 4:9, Paul exhorts with the character of love by proclaiming, *"The things you have learned and received and heard and seen...practice these things."*[2] We see clearly that diligently waiting is far from a passive, uncontrollable wish.

This whole book has been committed to this exercise. Relationships the way God intended them have very little to do with the external forces on our lives: Who will it be? Where will we meet? How will it happen? When will it happen? Godly relationships have everything to do with the internal restructuring God desires us to embrace. Take his truth and do it. Don't stop at hearing it, agreeing with it, talking about it, or theoretically proving it. Let those aspects be the catalyst to obediently, practically, with endurance, diligently doing it.

I am so encouraged and excited for those of you who have made it here. We must realize this is not the end but simply part of the process. Those who will diligently wait on the Lord will discover the fulfilling marriage He has in store.

What lies ahead?

Well, there is hard news and great news. If you have not yet discovered, the process is not easy and the complete results are not instantaneous. Philippians 1:6 is my admonition to you as you strive for God's best with all your heart, *"He who began a good work in you will perfect it until the day of Christ Jesus."*[3]

There will be times where nothing seems to be going right as you apply these truths. Take heart. That simply means it is working. Waiting diligently means we will not always bring the right order to the table every time. God is the most patient, understanding customer. Reproof is part of the process. Proverbs 12:1 puts it best, *"Whoever loves discipline, loves knowledge, but he who hates reproof is stupid."*[4] That is the hard news.

Now for the great news. The results are promised by the only one who can keep such promises. When we commit our lives to diligently waiting upon Him, He makes us some pretty awesome guarantees. Those who wait upon the Lord will gain new strength (Is. 40:31). Those who abide in the perfect truth of God will be blessed...(James 1:25).Through prayer and practice we are promised we will have the protection and peace of God (Phil. 4:6-7).

As the faithful Lord of all continues to refine your heart and life, revisit these truths regularly. Review what you have written and see the growth that is taking place.

Thank you for allowing me to be a part of your process. My prayer is for God to continue to mold you into becoming worthy of the love desire

[1]NAS
[2]NAS
[3]NAS
[4]NAS

RECONNECTING

Discussion / Action

1. What is the worst service you have ever received?

2. Put into your own words the idea of diligently waiting.

3. What truth or aspect of this book has been the most enjoyable?

4. What is one way you have attempted to change?

5. Name something you will take from this book an continue to apply in your life and/or marriage?

One Month Homework:

Read I Corinthians 13:4-7 and focus on one attribute each day. Make a concerted effort to show that quality to your spouse. Realize that you are a greater lover just because you are trying. God Bless